WRESTLING THE DRAGON

How I Fought Diabetes and Won

A memoir by
AJ Cunder

Disclaimer:

THE INFORMATION PROVIDED IN THIS BOOK IS NOT INTENDED TO REPLACE THE ADVICE AND COUNSEL OF A PROFESSIONAL MEDICAL PRACTITIONER. DO NOT START, STOP, OR OTHERWISE CHANGE A TREATMENT REGIMEN WITHOUT FIRST CONSULTING WITH YOUR PHYSICIAN.

I have attempted to recreate events, locales, and conversations as accurately as possible from my memory of them or as they were related to me by individuals directly involved. Although I have made every effort to ensure that the information presented in this book was correct at press time, I do not assume and hereby disclaim any liability to any party for any loss, damage, or disruption caused by errors or omissions, whether such errors or omissions resulted from negligence, accident, or any other cause.

Book design by AJ Cunder
Cover design © by AJ Cunder

Printed in the United States of America
First printing, 2017

www.WrestlingTheDragon.com

#ThisIsDiabetes

#diabetes

#T1D

#5KADA

#LiveBeyond

#DiabetesAtlas

#ArtificialPancreas

#JDRF

#WrestlingTheDragon

#DiabetesAwareness

#insulin

#T1DLooksLikeMe

#JDRFOneConference

#healthcare

#DiabetesStrong

#T2D

#DiabetesVoice

#StopDiabetes

"*Wrestling the Dragon* brings the reader inside the on-going daily battles of living with a chronic disease. AJ Cunder, diagnosed with Type I diabetes at age 17 months, shares his experiences – the 'highs' and the 'lows' – with compelling honesty, humor, courage and optimism. Anyone reading this book will find pearls of wisdom to fight one's personal 'dragon' from this young, talented author."

--*Johanna Burani MS, RD, CDE, author of #1 diet book* Good Carbs, Bad Carbs

Dedication / Acknowledgments

I would first like to dedicate this book to the millions of diabetics across America and around the world who suffer each day as they fight the dragon that lives inside them. I feel your pain. I know your struggle. I battle the beast each day alongside you, and I hope this book can at least bring you some consolation with the knowledge that you are not alone as you don your armor and prepare your lance in war against the dragon.

Secondly, I dedicate this book to my parents, whose lives changed forever when the dragon visited our family. They were the first to battle the beast, and taught me what I needed to know to continue the fight. Every night my father woke to check my blood sugar, every injection my mother gave me, every time she had to come to my elementary school and bring juice boxes, saltine crackers, refill my supply box, I thank them.

Thirdly, to Kyle and all spouses, boyfriends, and girlfriends of diabetics who know intimately our daily struggles. For supporting us, encouraging us, reminding us to take our basal shots or waking us up in the middle of the night when our sweat turns the bed into a pool because of a low blood sugar—I thank you. Although we may be strong by ourselves, fighting the dragon is always easier when we have someone like you at our side.

And finally, to all the medical care providers, doctors, nurses, endocrinologists, dieticians, and researchers who work each day to make our lives better and easier. A special thanks to the American Diabetes Association and the Juvenile Diabetes Research Foundation who strive tirelessly to find a cure and bring us all one step closer to a world without the dragon.

Table of Contents

Preface

When I say that I fought diabetes and won, I don't mean that I have somehow cured myself. Indeed, the dragon is still very much alive inside of me. When I say that I have beaten the dragon, I mean that I have learned how to conquer the dragon without ever getting rid of it. Diabetes is a part of my life, as it has and always will be until the day that science discovers a cure, but I do not let it control me. Yes, there are routines and habits I must practice because of my disease, but I have never let those define me or hold me back from pursuing my dreams and reaching out for my goals.

Certainly, diabetes has presented an obstacle to those goals, in some cases more drastically than others—the next chapter recounts such an instance. But I've learned how to persevere; how to press on, through and past the dragon that would stand in my way, breathing its hot fire.

I've recently joined diabetes support groups on Facebook, and my heart breaks when I read stories about diabetics struggling—when I see pictures posted of diabetics comatose in the hospital, or cries for help from diabetics who are tired of battling their disease. I want this book to be a story of hope for everyone out there who thinks that things will never get better; for diabetics who think that the dragon must control them; diabetics who think that a normal life is impossible; for Jenni A. who describes another diabetic shaming her for what she ate; for Kelsie P. and her daughter who was diagnosed with diabetes; for Allyy B. and all diabetics on blood-sugar roller coaster rides; for the 415 million people out there battling the dragon living inside them.

So if you've picked up this book—if you are a diabetic, newly diagnosed or a battle-hardened veteran—if you love a diabetic, know a diabetic, are struggling with the diagnosis of a child or a friend—if you want to know what it's like to wrestle the dragon, then read on and follow my path through childhood, adulthood, and everything in between while I carried the burden of the beast.

When the Dragon Nearly

Won

I had a dream, once, of becoming a Special Agent. As a kid, I'd run around the house with my cousin pretending to investigate crimes, arrest my dad and my uncle, and introduce myself as Special Agent Cunder. I fantasized about working for the FBI, and even took the Special Agent Entrance Exam in 2016. I passed, but I didn't have the two years of full time work experience the FBI requires for Special Agent applicants. And so I thought my dream would be on hold for a while, until I received an email from the United States Secret Service inviting me to take their Special Agent Entrance Examination. I had almost forgotten that I applied, and my heart jumped when I read the email. Could this be it? I wondered. Could this be my path? The road that will take me to my dream of becoming a Special Agent with the federal government?

I'd have to go to Brooklyn to take the test. Either that or

Washington, D.C., but I lived in New Jersey so I chose Brooklyn. I wondered if the test would be like the FBI's. They offered a preparation guide online, and it gave an overview of the sections: Logic-based reasoning, Experience Inventory, Language Usage, Detail Observation where I'd have a few minutes to study a photograph and then remember as many details about it to answer questions like how many pieces of paper were hanging from the bulletin board, or what was written on the open box sitting on the floor in front of the cabinets, all without looking back at the photo.

I studied. And studied. And prepared. The day came, and I dressed in my suit, shoved my glucose monitor in my front pocket and tucked the note from my doctor next to it (in case they questioned why I needed insulin and glucose tablets). I made sure to take my bottle of orange juice in case my blood sugar started to drop, slipping it in its customary niche (back-left pants pocket) and set out on the train, resume and folder nestled under my arm.

I got there about an hour early and found the restroom where I'd go to check my blood sugar about five times before the test began, balancing my monitor on a wobbly roll of toilet paper. I wanted to make sure I wasn't high or low, that I was completely focused and that the dragon wouldn't distract me.

In the lobby of the Brooklyn Marriott, I sunk into a leather chair, watching businessmen and women congregate around the bar or rush to the elevators, wondering if any of the passing suits were Secret Service Agents preparing to administer the exam. I looked for guns or badges, tried to see if they had an earpiece like the Agents in movies. Soon, other applicants began to fill in the chairs around me, their suits pressed, their hair cut short, some kids in their twenties like me, others bordering thirty. Would any of us make it through the whole process? Would I see any of these people again at the academy, if I got hired? Could this day be the start of my career?

Finally, a Uniformed Division Officer in a black polo and tactical pants summoned us to the ballroom where we would take our test. I swallowed. Was I ready? They checked our bags and pockets for weapons. I showed my note when the officer with the metal detector wand raised an eyebrow at my blue and orange insulin pen. "I'm a diabetic," I explained.

"Oh, okay," she said. "No problem."

Then we filed into the seats at the rows of tables, every other to prevent the urge to cheat. "If anyone needs the restroom before we start, you'll be escorted out and back by an agent," one woman said. She wasn't an agent, just a representative from the Secret Service's Talent and Employee Acquisition Management Division. The minutes ticked by. And then we were given our test booklets. Our pencils. Our instructions.

Of course, I'm not at liberty to say what the test contained. I'm bound to secrecy about much of the application process by a non-disclosure agreement. Don't worry, government agents reading this: everything I say can be readily found online.

The test was difficult. Afterwards, even though I got straight A's in high school, graduated with a 3.99 GPA from college and a 4.0 from graduate school, I wasn't entirely certain I had passed. When Jaqcueline Wasson, the woman from the TAD (Talent and Employee Acquisition Management Division), returned from grading the exams and gave the results to a Uniformed Division Officer (he was a sergeant, I believe). He started calling out names, summoning candidates to the back of the room where they were escorted out. Every time a name started with an *A*, my pulse quickened. "Anthony," he started to call out, and my gut clenched, but he didn't say *Cunder*. He called someone else. And when he finally stopped calling names, someone behind me said, "Holy shit." Half of the room had cleared out, and we started with about 150 applicants.

Special Agent Susan Goggin, a chief recruiting officer for the Secret Service, came into the room and congratulated us, told us we were the ones who passed, and gave us a Realistic Job briefing. She explained what we could expect from a career as a Secret Service Special Agent and what the rest of the application process would entail. I thought about what it would actually be like, serving the country as an agent, seeing things that "other people would never have the opportunity to see," as SA Goggin put it. The tingle of anticipation crawled through my veins. But I still had a lot left to get through before I made it there. Before I made it to the Federal Law Enforcement Training Center and then the Secret Service's John J. Rowling Training Center where I'd complete the academy. I still had my panel interview, my security interview, my background check, my medical exam. But SA Goggin and Ms. Wasson said something that gave me hope: I would only be competing with myself throughout the application process, and if I passed everything, a job would be waiting for me at the end. So many times before I had passed phases in an application process only to be told that another, more qualified candidate had been selected over me. But not this time. This time, as long as I passed, I would get hired, and that gave me such sweet, tantalizing hope.

We signed up for our interview dates. This was an expedited process, SA Goggin said, with an estimated time frame (for successful candidates) of three-to-four months from the date of the written test to getting the phone call with reporting instructions for the beginning of our training class. The interviews would take place in the D.C. area with four available dates: two in late November, two in early December. I wanted to move through the process as quickly as possible, so I signed up for November 20th and prepared myself for the questions they'd ask, reviewing my work history, situations in which I had demonstrated integrity, my problem-solving skills, and my ability to work in a team.

The enthusiastic *"Passed the SS test"* texts went out to friends and family as I checked Google Maps on my phone and navigated to the nearest subway station. I told my dad to get ready for a trip to D.C. Whether he wanted to or not, I was dragging him down there for the ride.

I got an email about a week before my interview date with more detailed instructions. It also said that, for those who passed the oral interview, the security interview would immediately follow. It could be an eight-hour day for successful candidates, so I told my dad to make sure he brought reading material if he planned to stay at the motel.

We made the trip (his girlfriend Donna came along with us too), checked into our rooms, searched for a decent place to eat. Nothing in the strip mall next to the Red Roof Inn looked appealing—a sketchy restaurant that didn't even look like it was open, a grocery store, and a pizza place where the cashier behind the counter was more concerned with his phone conversation then with acknowledging the customers trying to order a slice. We eventually found a Denny's within driving distance, and I tried to eat, even though my stomach was roiling. I always hated interviews. I hated talking about myself. I never sold myself the way everyone said I should. I thought about what a wasted trip this would be—a waste of a weekend and a four-to-five-hour drive if I didn't pass.

"But at least you'll get experience," my dad said as I tried to swallow my pancakes.

"You're going to drop me off there in the morning, right?" I made sure. "I have to be there at six-forty-five, so we should probably leave by like six-fifteen. It's only about ten minutes away, but still, I'd rather make sure I'm early."

"Absolutely, always better to be early," he said.

"And I told you it could be up to eight hours, right? If I pass the interview." Another sip of green tea to calm my nerves. "If I text you sooner, that means I didn't pass."

"You'll pass. But I'll keep my phone on."

I took a shower, slipped between those cool, crisp sheets so unique to cheap motels, and we watched something on TV before getting to sleep early. It took me a while to doze off, with everything running through my mind. What my future would be like as a Special Agent (if I passed). What it would feel like to get that badge, to finally achieve my childhood dream. The responsibility of protecting the President, the First Family, members of Congress, important people whose lives would be entrusted to me. Tossing this way and that, I stripped off my shirt, my shorts to find a comfortable temperature. It felt like hours before the void claimed me, and then minutes before my alarm clanged like an otherworldly summons. A quick shave. Checked my sugar—74 mg/dl—took a few sips of Gatorade, but not too much since I tended to run high in the morning. Especially with added stress. I put on my suit. Straightened my tie. Checked the map on my phone once more. Stuffed my attaché case with snacks and more Gatorade, my insulin and glucometer.

"Good luck, Age," my dad said. "Just remember, be confident."

"I know. You keep saying that. It's not like I can just *be confident*, though. I get nervous. Just stop talking about it," I said with an edge. I didn't want to be reminded of how nervous interviews always made me. I just wanted to get it over with. Soon, I kept telling myself. Whatever the outcome, soon it would be over and I could move on.

We drove down the deserted streets at 6:30 AM, to the Secret Service's dedicated training center. "You're here for the applicant interviews?" the Officer at the security gate said.

"Yes." I showed him my driver's license like the email instructed.

"Are you staying with him or just dropping off?" he asked my dad.

"Just dropping him off."

"Drive up to that van there and then get out. They'll do a sweep of your car, and then you take a right. You'll see the parking lot ahead. Then come back out this way."

"Sweep of the car?" my dad said under his breath as we pulled through the gate.

"Maybe they want to make sure you don't have a bomb or drugs? This is a government facility." The thought excited me. Gave me a thrill that I might one day soon be a part of this secure, secret government organization. That I would get to live a life others only saw in movies.

We got out, and the canine officers led their dogs around the car. "Okay, you're good to go," they said finally.

One final time, my dad wished me "Good luck," and I walked with my satchel in hand weighed down by my supplies for wrestling the dragon along with the massive packet of security clearance forms required for my Factor V interview—should I pass the first stage. I tried calming my nerves, but of course that's always impossible. I checked in, gave a printed copy of my resume, showed my driver's license again. I was the fourth applicant to arrive. Secret Service employees brought us to a room, made us wait. Others filtered in. Ms. Wasson was there. They shuffled through paperwork, sifted through our resumes. Called the first three out, led them away. I waited. When would they call me?

"Anthony Cunder?" they said. "This way." They led me into the hall, to a small room with lights that kept clicking off. Two agents sat at a table, looking back at me, one typing at a computer. What was he typing? He paused to rub his eye.

"Something in your eye?" the other said. "Do you need to go to the bathroom?"

"No, a twenty might help me get it though," he said looking at me with his hand outstretched.

I laughed, genuinely amused by the joke, and they laughed too. A good way to start things off.

Then they went over a list of things—automatic disqualifiers they called it—asking if I had used illegal drugs before coming there (they'd seen it before, they said, don't think that one's a joke), or if I'd ever been convicted of a felony. Some questions needed an affirmative response, like whether or not I'd be willing to work unscheduled shifts, or travel overseas, so they told me to make sure I listened to each question carefully (some people just said "No," because they thought that's what they were supposed to say). I listened, and I answered, and then we moved on to the important part: the part where I'd have to talk about myself, where they asked...

Well, I can't tell you what they asked. Non-disclosure agreement and all. But by the end I felt like I had done well. They asked if I had any questions, and I asked them about their careers, what they liked best and what they found to be difficult about the job. I asked if they had any advice for me, and they said that they felt I would do well in the New York field office (where I'd be stationed if I was extended a final job offer) because I was from the area and knew how to deal with people from New York. I was already a police officer in Union City, and knew how to command a crowd when necessary. I had the experience. That gave me confidence. I shook their hands, and they directed me to wait out in the hall where someone came and escorted me to the first room where I held my breath and let myself hope.

I watched the other applicants, listened to the talk amongst each other, looked sidelong at a kid sitting next to me. Did he take his interview? Did he pass?

Near the front table littered with paperwork, where they had my application packet, I heard someone say, "We have two for the Factor V." Was I one of the two?

Yes, I was. Someone came and escorted me to the next phase as a sensation of euphoria coursed through me like the air just before a lightning strike. I had passed the hardest part, I thought. Everything from here on would be cake. The interview, in past applications with local police agencies, was where I usually tripped up. From here, it would all be downhill.

I breezed through the Security Interview (my record was clean—never even got a traffic ticket) and then went on to schedule my polygraph exam for December 2, 2016 at 2:00 PM. Then I texted my dad, told him to come pick me up. Only a few hours had passed. It was only 9:10.

You can come get me, I sent.

OK.

Should I go into that same building and I tell them I'm picking you up

Should I tell them that we're going to check out today
Yea we can check out today
But come get me first

The applicant coordinators asked if I drove or if I was getting picked up. I said my ride was on its way. They said I couldn't wait there, so they'd walk me out to the front security gate. I could wait there for my dad, they said. I called him, made sure he was coming. It was cold, and I didn't have my coat. Thankfully, he pulled in as I got to the front. I shook hands with the Uniformed Division Officer manning the post, and I saw Donna sitting in the back.

"You can sit up front," she said as I got in and warmed my hands by the heating vents. I didn't say anything as we pulled out onto the road. I'm sure my dad was thinking about what to say.

"You know, Age, I'm proud of you. You passed the test, you came down here. I'm sure there were a lot of qualified people, and I'm proud of you for making it this far."

"But I passed," I said, my chuckle bubbling through my smirk. "I have my polygraph scheduled for December second."

"You passed? You creep!" he laughed. "I thought you said it would be bad news if we came to get you early."

"Oh congratulations!" Donna said from the back.

"Wow, yes, congratulations! I told you you're the best candidate."

"Yeah, I thought it would be bad news too, that's what they said in the email. But I was there early, so I got through everything pretty quick. I'm sure there are still people there who will take the full eight hours."

"See, always a good thing to get there early," my dad said, along with more praise and congratulatory remarks.

We called my uncle—he always said he had a good feeling about the Secret Service, and he was himself an Officer with U.S. Customs and Border Protection. He thought, too, that if we called him early that would mean I didn't pass. So my dad called him, and I said hi. The sympathy in his voice was so thick, I almost felt bad tricking him. Almost. He and my dad talked for a while, and then we told him that I had my polygraph on December second.

The relief and amazement that streamed through the phone was nearly tangible. "Age, you got me good!" he said. "I was totally stunned, I'm telling you. You got me. But congratulations! Now just get through the polygraph."

He had heard horror stories, though, about the polygraph. He knew a few of the polygraph examiners for U.S. Customs, and they told him the failure rate was usually seventy percent for applicants. I heard stories too, about people who failed just because they were nervous, so of course, I got nervous too, even though I knew my background was clean. Drug use was the number one reason for polygraph failure, and I had nothing to worry about there. I'd never even seen a marijuana joint before I started working in law enforcement.

Again, the texts went out. *Passed SS interview*, I told my friends and family.

I got an email with a conditional offer of employment, and I couldn't help but smile as I read it over and over again. A conditional job offer for the career of my dreams. I can hardly describe the feeling.

At work, I told my sergeant about the process, told my fellow officers, not overly confident just yet but letting myself hope more and more.

I got a new suit—gray—and wore that on the day of my polygraph. I met with another applicant in the lobby of the Secret Service building in Brooklyn, and I told him about the seventy-percent failure rate. He started to look a little nervous, and when I saw him leave early—when the other three of us got a break—I felt a little guilty. He didn't look happy. I hope I wasn't the reason why he failed.

Again, I can't say exactly what happened during the polygraph examination. That's all classified information.

But it was three hours long, and grueling. The interrogating agent asked me about every facet of my life and background, picking it all apart. Hundreds of questions while hooked up to feet pads, butt pads, heart rate monitors, pneumatic monitors, all the while remaining perfectly still, staring at the opposite wall. It was not a pleasant experience. Even the sergeant who spoke with me during my Security Interview said that his polygraph exam was one of the worst experiences of his life, and it's even worse for applicants with perfectly clean records because the interviewers are disinclined to believe them.

But I got through it. Question by question, I passed. The agent told me that the results would be sent to Washington where an independent review panel would verify the results. She asked if I would be okay with coming back for additional testing if they found any discrepancies, and I said yes. What else could I say? I asked about a time frame moving forward. She said it could move very quickly, if Washington wanted to push applicants through before the holidays, or a bit longer if they decided to wait. She wasn't sure.

So I left, texted everyone again, and waited, daring to hope that I would soon live my dream.

The process did move quickly. Less than a week later, on

December 8, 2016, I received a phone call from Special Agent Darrel Goss who was completing the New Jersey portion of my background investigation. He wanted to set up a time to come to my apartment for my "home interview" where he and his boss would sit down with me and discuss any issues in my background, talk about the job in greater detail, and see if I had any questions about what a Special Agent career with the Secret Service would entail.

I was at work when I received the call, at the Alternative Design Academy where I was assigned as a School Resource Officer. I told Tony Sciavicco, one of the security guards there, along with Joe Chieco (another security guard) and Pat Campen (a teacher). I told them that I pretty much had the job, at this point. My background was clean—I had no concerns there—and the only step after that would be the medical exam. My pulse skyrocketed, and I believed that day that I would soon become a Special Agent with the Secret Service—that all my years of searching for a job would culminate in this blissful moment of getting the phone call from Washington, congratulating me for being among the top one-percent of applicants, and telling me when to report to the Federal Law Enforcement Training Center in Georgia. My co-workers congratulated me. They patted me on the back. They said I deserved this, after trying for so long and searching so intently for the right career.

I got another phone call the next day to schedule my medical exam in Manhattan. I was assigned December 12, the following Monday. I received a confirmation email with a packet of forms I was required to complete and bring with me, asking about every aspect of my medical history. I explained that I had type I diabetes (well-controlled) with a strict treatment regimen. I worried about it slightly, but I had passed prior law enforcement medical reviews (one for the Essex County Sheriff's Office and another for the Union City Police Department). I had my doctor fill out some forms I had from another medical exam I took for a position with U.S. Customs and Border Protection that verified my ability to perform the essential job functions of a federal law enforcement officer. I could make quick decisions. I could work extended hours and prolonged shifts, drive vehicles with responsibility for others. I could be a Special Agent with the United States Secret Service.

I took all the paperwork from my doctor with me on that day in December, even though the Secret Service didn't explicitly ask for it. I wanted to be proactive. I didn't want them to come back and say I didn't support my ability to do the job with the proper documentation. I met with the physician from the Federal Occupational Health center and told her I had diabetes. She said she didn't expect that to be a problem. I passed every aspect of the exam without an issue: the hearing test, eyesight exam, blood work, EKG. I knew I was in optimal health. I exercised nearly every day. I had an "athlete's pulse," one nurse commented. And I left the facility confident that my condition would not stand in the way of my dreams.

I spoke with Special Agent Goss the next day at my apartment. My dad was there too (turns out SA Goss's supervisor recognized my father from Assumption Parish in Morristown, NJ where my dad serves as a Eucharistic Minister). SA Goss explained what the training for the Special Agent position would be like, and asked if I was willing to commit myself to this career; to work long hours away from home, stand at security posts during the holidays, endure inclement weather. "Yes," I told him. "This is my dream. I'm willing to do anything for this job."

He expected the process to move quickly from that point forward. "You might get a phone call as soon as two weeks," he said, "or possibly as late as March." I told him I applied through the expedited process, and he again was confident that I'd get a phone call soon. "We're actively hiring," he said. "We definitely need agents."

For the next few days, my heart jumped every time my

phone rang. Could this be it? I wondered. Could this be the phone call I've waited for, I've dreamt about, I've wanted ever since I was a kid?

Days turned into weeks that slowly rolled into months. When March came and I still hadn't heard anything, I called the Secret Service trying to get a status update. *No further action is required*, the email reply said. *You are currently being processed.*

When would I hear something? I figured that maybe the inauguration had something to do with it, pushing everything back a few months. But this long?

Then on March 28, 2017 I received a phone call from my dad. He had seen the Special Agent who recognized him during my home interview. They spoke after 12PM mass at Assumption Parish. He asked my dad if I had received a letter from the Secret Service. That something had come up in my medical exam. He asked my dad if I had any other employment prospects available.

And my heart nearly stopped.

Could diabetes really crush my dreams?

Could the prejudice of the Secret Service against otherwise qualified individuals with disabilities really stand in the way of my career?

I wanted to cry. To curl up in a ball and throw my phone

out the window. But I couldn't. I was working, posted at an Elementary School in Union City, and I couldn't let my emotions get in the way of my job.

I prayed that my grandmother who had passed years ago would intercede for me, would ask God to let me hear something, anything from the Secret Service. An hour later, I got an email from a nurse consultant asking for additional medical information to assist in the processing of my medical review. I nearly collapsed with relief. I was still in the running. I still had a chance.

The paperwork asked me to write detailed responses to questions about my medical history, how I control my condition, treatment plans, physical fitness activities, how I could handle the physical and mental stresses of the position, whether I had passed previous medical examinations, my history of occupational firearms qualifications. I explained that I have kept my diabetes tightly controlled, that my A1C values had ranged between 6.3 and 6.8 consistently for the past ten years, that I have never had a severe incident of hypo or hyperglycemia. That my diabetes had not once in the past four years ever interfered with my work as a law enforcement officer.

I sent the documents, signed, dated, and emailed.

And heard nothing for a week. Two weeks. I tried calling

Jacqueline Thomas-Vincent several times until she finally answered. I asked if she received the documents I sent, and she said she didn't see them. So I tried again, and asked if she would please send me a reply so I'd know they went through. Didn't hear from her again, so I tried the next day. *Good Afternoon*, she wrote on April 12, 2017 *I do apologize that I did not respond to your email but I did receive them and have already forwarded them for processing. Thanks!!*

And then the weeks rolled by. Still I heard nothing. So I called, and emailed, asking for an update, something, anything to help ease my mind, and on April 24, 2017, I received a phone call that crushed me. Physically. Mentally. Emotionally. Spiritually. That made me feel as though the floor gave out underneath my feet and I fell into a dark abyss.

A nurse consultant called me and said that I would be receiving a letter in the next few weeks regarding the status of my medical review. I asked her why I would be receiving a letter, as my knowledge of the application process was that written forms of notification would only be used for applicants who did not pass a certain phase. She asked if I had ever taken and/or passed a pre-employment medical examination before. I answered yes, I had, both for the local police department where I worked as a Class II Police Officer and for the Essex County Sheriff's Office where I served as a deputy sheriff. She stated that local police agency medical reviews are easier to pass (for people with disabilities) than the federal government's. She then stated that there were certain problems with my medical paperwork. She said that my blood glucose, when tested at the Federal Occupational Health clinic during my physical examination, was 192 mg/dl and that was "abnormal." I reiterated that I was a diabetic, and that no diabetic, no matter how tight his control, can experience perfect blood glucose 100% of the time, and that I do occasionally experience isolated incidents of elevated blood glucose. I informed her that my latest A1C value, tested on April 17, 2017, which measures an individual's average blood glucose over the previous three months, was 6.8%. This is within the American Diabetes Association's recommended value of under 7.0% for adults with tightly controlled diabetes. I also informed her that I have never had an A1C value above 7.0% for the past ten years, an indication of my excellent level of blood glucose control. I offered to email my medical records for review, but she refused.

I told her that if the Secret Service discriminated against me solely on the basis of my diabetes diagnoses, then I would pursue legal remedies. That such action was the definition of disability discrimination, and I was aware of a few other cases where diabetics had sued the federal government for rejecting their Special Agent applications: Kapche v. Holder, who sued the FBI and won; Branham v. Snow, who sued the IRS and won. But she didn't care. The Secret Service didn't care. She said it was a competitive position. Why should the Secret Service hire a diabetic when there are plenty of other applicants who don't have a disability? she asked me.

Why should we hire you?

Why should they hire me....

It felt like my world was ending. My hopes and dreams that had taken flight just a few short months ago now crashed back to earth like falling stars, aimed straight at my head. I was at my uncle's when I got that phone call. Thank God I was around family, or I don't know what I would have done. I nearly got lost on my way home—a trip I had taken so many times before. I missed the turn. Took some dark, deserted back roads and eventually got to where I needed to go. And my mind wandered, my anger festered. How could the Secret Service do this to me? It wasn't official yet, though, I reasoned. I hoped. I prayed. I still might make it. They still might do the right thing.

After all, one of Jeff Kapche's attorneys said on her law firm's website, "Kapche is a powerful example that a medical condition does not dictate your ability to be successful in any field you choose. Because of Jeff Kapche and his legal team, others with diabetes no longer need to check their dreams at the door."

But I did have to check my dreams. On May 18, 2017, I got the email that turned my knees to water and ripped my heart out of my chest. *Dear Ms. Cunder*, it began—yes, they called me *Ms.* They couldn't even get the honorific right. *This is to advise you of the action taken on your application for the position of Special Agent with the U.S. Secret Service.*

The Secret Service Reviewing Physician has advised that your medical documentation shows that you have Type I diabetes mellitus. According to the medical report dated December 12, 2016, you are required to use medications to control your condition. A Special Agent's job involves unexpectedly prolonged and rotational work shifts, frequent international travel, and a possibility of assignment to a relatively austere environment. The work conditions and requirements of a Special Agent significantly increase the likelihood for aggravation, exacerbation, or worsening of your condition. Your condition also places you at significant risk of hypoglycemic event. After a careful review, the Secret Service Reviewing Physician has determined that you do not meet the standards for the Special Agent position.

For the first time in my life, diabetes—the dragon living within me—stood in the way of my dreams.

I spoke to an attorney. He said I had a strong claim for disability discrimination. So I went through the motions, gathered all of my emails from the Secret Service, compiled a timeline of events. But even litigation wouldn't fix the hole in my heart. Nothing could soothe the pain I felt, the desolation of coming so far—reaching the finish line—and then getting tripped because of something inside me that I cannot change. Did they even read the medical documentation I sent them? The paperwork from my doctor? Or was that all just a formality, something to string me along, give me hope when really, there was no hope. This whole process was just a waste of time because I'm a diabetic and they already knew they'd disqualify me because of it, in blatant defiance of the American Rehabilitation Act—the Americans with Disabilities Act—because of their own prejudice and blindness.

Maybe litigation will work. If not for me, then for the other diabetics across the country who face discrimination because of the dragon inside them. If I have to be an example—like Kapche and those before him—so that other diabetics don't have to feel the humiliation and disappointment that the Secret Service has made me feel, then I'll accept that sacrifice. And just because the Secret Service rejected me, that doesn't mean I'll give up. I won't let the dragon win. My dreams might have been crushed for now, but I'll keep working. I'll keep striving. I'll set my sights on the FBI, an agency that *has* hired diabetic applicants as Special Agents, and keep working toward that goal.

I won't let my diabetes win. I won't let the dragon win.

It may have stymied me for the moment—it may have won this battle—but I will never give up until I win the war.

PART I

❧❧❧❧ ✖ ✻ ✖ ❧❧❧❧

DISCOVERING THE BEAST

The Dragon's Birth

Every diabetic's story about how we met the dragon is different. Like how we met our spouse, or boyfriend, or girlfriend, or significant other, how we met the beast that came to live inside us is unique. Some of us met the dragon at ten years old, or fifteen, or thirty. Others when we were infants. Some of us had family members—fathers, mothers, brothers, sisters—who fought the dragon and so they were on guard, always watching for the moment when the dragon would visit them too. Some discovered the dragon during a routine doctor's visit, a simple blood test that would change their lives forever. And others nearly died before they learned about the dragon, suffering and tormented for days or weeks before a doctor finally thought to check them for diabetes.

That was my story. I nearly died before my parents learned about the dragon that changed everything. I was only seventeen months old when the diagnosis came, and while I don't remember any of it, of course, I asked my parents what it was like. From what they've told me, it went something like this:

The week of February 20, 1994.

The shaggy blue carpet of 52 Regina Place tickled my toes as I waddled across the floor, my arms stretched out toward my mother. I latched onto her leg, hugging it tightly. "Bobby!" I said.

"You want your bottle?" my mom cooed, her voice soft and comforting. "Let go of my leg, and I'll get it for you." She smiled, her curly hair falling around her tan face despite the winter months. I gripped her leg more fervently, and she gently prised me off, handing me my bottle. I gulped it down, and five minutes later asked for it again, drinking more in a single day than I would in a week. A glint of concern flashed in my mother's eye as she filled my bottle for the third time. A trickle of urine ran down my leg, soaking through the diaper.

"Is this normal?" she asked my dad in a whisper as I slept that night.

He rubbed his strong jaw, his face stern, his dark brown eyes watching me, following the steady rise and fall of my chest. A sliver of light snuck past the nearly-closed door, landing on my face as I lay in my crib. "I don't think so," he answered, a gruff rumble that overpowered the stillness of the room. I fidgeted under my blanket, and the blue and pink mobile revolved overhead, the soft chime of "Twinkle-Twinkle-Little-Star" struggling to continue, draining whatever energy remained in the toy before it died out.

In the morning, my mom returned, reached into the crib and lifted me with a smile. "Good morning, sleepy head!"

I giggled a bit, but my lips had acquired a bluish tinge. She put me down, and I tried to walk across the room to my treasure chest of toys. But I couldn't get to it. I tried to walk. I had walked yesterday. I'd learned how to walk months ago. But I stumbled. I fell. I crawled, barely scraping along the floor, trying to get to my toys. My arms gave out, and I collapsed, barely breathing. A crystal tear leaked from my mother's eye and rolled to the corner of her mouth. She scooped me up and held me in her arms while she walked to the kitchen.

"Robin?" She called one of her friends, pinning the phone to her ear with her shoulder. "It's Dolores."

Robin offered a greeting of some sort. "Hey listen," my mom went on, "AJ has been acting kind of strange lately." She listed my odd behavior.

"Well of course he's peeing a lot. What do you expect with how much he's drinking?"

"But what about the walking? He was fine just last

week."

"I couldn't tell you, Dee. Maybe you should take him to a doctor."

"I don't want to make it more than it is, if it's nothing. You know Anthony doesn't like doctors. He thinks AJ might catch another bug. He already had something this month. I thought he was over it."

"That could be why he's losing weight. Or maybe he's just going through some kind of growth spurt."

"Not like any kind of growth spurt I've ever seen. His diapers are so big they just slip right off sometimes. It's like they... Do you really think this could happen just from a cold?"

"Could be," Robin says. "Don't really know what to tell you, though." They chatted for a while longer.

On Thursday or Friday of that week, my parents finally decided to take me to my pediatrician. Dr. Lipat gave me a routine check: eyes, ears, nose, throat. "Nothing wrong," he said. "He's just recovering from something going around. He was sick earlier in the month, right?"

My parents nodded. "Are you sure that's all this is?" they asked.

"Quite sure. Nothing wrong that I can see," he affirmed.

So they took me home, and a few more days went by.

to my open mouth, bits of orange mush dribbling down my chin. My Aunt Karen looked at Grandma Pat, then asked my mom if she's been feeding me.

Mom glared at her and said, "Of course. He's just really hungry all the time." She didn't know that she was feeding the dragon. It was the dragon inside me that wanted food.

Grandma Pat took a closer look at my face, examining the dark circles under my eyes. "Maybe it's a vitamin deficiency," she suggested.

I ate more macaroni, this time with applesauce, until I slumped in the chair.

The house didn't seem to interest me the way it always had, my grandmother's collection of bells undisturbed and unstudied, the garage with its mysterious nooks and crannies unexplored. We left, and, just minutes from home, the dragon growled inside me. I threw up, spewing all over the car. Mom looked back and cried. At the house, she drew up a bath, scrubbing my face with a soft washcloth. I didn't splash. I didn't play with my plastic ships. I rested my head against the ceramic tub and closed my eyes, barely breathing.

She called the doctor again and left a message with the emergency line, taking the medical book into the bathroom. Sitting on the toilet, she wrapped her hair around her fingers.

A tear dripped down the silky strands, staining the white pages.

The phone rang, and she jumped to answer it. She mentioned I had thrown up. The doctor sighed. "Just recovering from a bug. He had an upset stomach earlier in the month, didn't he? Just give him Gatorade, and we'll see him tomorrow." He disconnected.

She called my dad. "Get some Gatorade on your way home."

Into my "bobby" the orange Gatorade went. I took a few sips, then spat it out. The bottle fell from my hand. The dragon growled. I think it wanted the Gatorade.

February 28, 1994—Monday.

The sun failed to penetrate the gray barrier of clouds, and the ice glittered on my dad's blue Monte Carlo.

We sat in the waiting room, the toys once so enticing left untouched. I didn't move much, just looked around with hollow eyes. The nurse called us into the examination room, and my parents lowered me onto the crinkling white paper. White lights flashed, and the charts and diagrams of human anatomy looked back at us. The doctor checked me again. Eyes. Ears. Nose. Throat. No temperature, no fever. Nothing wrong. Just the recurrence of a bug that's going around.

"Something is wrong," my dad said. "Check him again."

The doctor shook his head. "I've just checked. Nothing is wrong."

"Something is wrong," my dad repeated, his face getting red, his voice heated. "He's peeing a lot, drinking a lot, he can't walk and barely moves. Something is wrong!"

"No," Dr. Lipat began to say.

"Something is wrong!" When my dad gets angry, his eyes burn as though with hellfire. As though every ounce of rage and anger boil up inside him and radiate from his core, ravishing everything in his path. He took a step toward the doctor, his hands balled into fists.

Maybe my dad's eyes scared him. Maybe they didn't. Either way, Lipat went to a cabinet and pulled out a plastic cup with a contraption for collecting urine from a young child. "Have him pee in this tonight and bring it back tomorrow."

"We'll do it right now," my dad said. He took me to the bathroom, and I filled the cup.

The doctor looked at it, snapped the lid on, and smiled metallically. "We'll give this to the lab."

The seconds ticked by, becoming minutes. Minutes became five. Five became ten. Ten became fifteen. Finally,

Dr. Lipat returned. He frowned as he looked at my parents, rubbing the back of his neck. Then he said, "You need to take him to the hospital right away."

My dad's face turned crimson, and his fists trembled. "You said there was nothing wrong. You said he was fine. You —!"

Dr. Lipat recoiled, backing against the wall, his eyes wide. My mom grabbed my father's arm, and they rushed out of the office, back to the car, went home for a moment, packed a bag with some of my clothes and a few other essentials. Mom took me to the Emergency Room of Morristown Memorial Hospital; Dad said he'd be there soon.

The intake personnel assigned me a cubicle with curtains separating it from the corridor. The fluorescent lights shone cold and hard, one flickering intermittently as the adult-sized bed drowned me. Nurses came and checked my vitals: eyes, ears, nose, throat.

"Why are you doing this again?" my mother asked. "The doctor just checked all of this at the office!" Her lower lip quivered. Her eyes glistened.

"Routine procedure, ma'am. We don't know what the doctor did, so we have to check again."

They transferred me to another room, and my dad joined us. Wide, brown double doors opened into a stark corridor lined with stretchers. Patients walked, and doctors followed, each with their own problems. The bleak blue walls of my new room pressed in on us, a navy gurney waiting for me, the slab upon which I would be sacrificed to the beast.

Some doctors came. White coats. Shiny name badges. Silver stethoscopes. One pointed to another; a heavy-set woman. The first doctor said, "Start the IV."

She nodded and scuttled to the bedside. She jabbed the needle into my arm. Then took it out. Blood spurted up from my elbow, and I howled. Sweat popped up on my father's forehead despite the air conditioning. She tried again.

"Is everyone in this room a doctor?" my dad asked, wiping his forehead with a sleeve.

"Yes, yes, of course," the first doctor said. "Here, do it like this," he said to the woman.

"Wait!" my dad screamed. "Why are you telling her how to do it? Is she a doctor? Is she a doctor?" When the man hesitated, dad growled—more ferocious than any dragon. "You do it!" He thrust his finger into the man's chest. "Don't tell her what to do, *you* do it."

My mother sang to me, a lullaby perhaps.

"I think you'd better wait outside," the doctor told my father.

With the force of a hurricane, my father cried, "I won't

say it again, you do it!"

The woman cowered and backed away. The doctor put the needle in my arm. He and the other white coats left after connecting the machines, drawing blood, taking the necessary samples. It turned out that they were trainees. I was at a teaching hospital.

The staff put me in the Intensive Care Unit. The lights blazed even brighter there. The smells of alcohol, iodine, and sanitizer filled the air. My parents stayed with me until the doctors balanced the glucose in my blood—until the dragon calmed. Until I got the antidote that kept its fire at bay. The *beeps* of the monitors filled the void. White walls closed us in, shutting us out, squeezing my parents' hearts as I lay on the hospital bed, the slab, the dragon's altar. The beast's fire burned inside me, tubes and fluids coming in and out of my small body, my mind floating in the clouds.

Dr. Starkman finally came and spoke with my parents. The endocrinologist explained what the doctors had found: a blood glucose reading of over 500 mg/dl,[1] brain swelling, and severe dehydration.

I had type I juvenile diabetes.

My father asked Dr. Starkman why my pediatrician

---

[1] Blood glucose is often measured in milligrams per deciliter of blood. A normal range is between 80 – 100 mg/dl.

could have been so blind, could miss such common symptoms.

"Well," Dr. Starkman reasoned, "it's unusual for diabetes to be diagnosed at such an early age. He probably didn't think to check. Especially without any family history of it." So I was an anomaly.

He left, promising he'd come again soon.

Mom stayed: scared, sad, overwhelmed.

Dad went to Astoria to pick up my Great-Aunt Margie so she could stay with me in the hospital. He cursed life, God, the devil. He "felt like he was in hell." After trying to have a child for ten years, he now had to watch his only son teeter on the brink of death.

I remained in the I.C.U. for a few days. The worst days of my father's life, he says. My family visited, my parents cried. The dragon's fire is hot, and they felt it through me. My battle with the beast began that day as the dragon's poison burned through my veins. The day my life changed forever. February 28, 1994. My grandmother's birthday.

An Ally in the Fight

My earliest memories of diabetes are really the earliest memories I have of my childhood. Growing up with the dragon inside me made injections commonplace. Every day, I'd get a shot. Every day, my parents would check my blood sugar. I remember standing on this little plastic stool at our kitchen counter, holding out my arm across the cold granite as my dad would wipe my finger with the alcohol swab, prick me with the lancet, squeeze out the red drop of blood and we'd wait as the meter ticked down. Every day I had to watch what I ate, have my meals and snacks at the scheduled times, make sure I didn't go low. My parents managed everything for me. I would let them know if I started feeling weak or especially hungry, when the dragon started growling, and they'd get me my juice and crackers first, then check my sugar. I was right most of the time. It was like instinct, for me, knowing when my sugar was below normal. I knew the dragon well. If I couldn't get rid of it, I might as well get to know it as intimately as I could. Keep your friends close and your enemies closer, right?

As I approached the age of seven or eight, though, I

experienced something during my yearly physical that made me really hate having diabetes. Every year in January, my endocrinologist, Dr. Starkman, would schedule lab work which included drawing blood. Every year when that moment came—and even for the week leading up to it—the dragon writhed within me. "It's because of you that I need to do this every year," I told the beast. It just bared its teeth in a twisted smile as I broke out in cold sweats at night, dreading the moment when the needle would pierce my arm, puncture my vein, suck the blood out of my body like a vampire.

I tried everything I possibly could to avoid that visit. Pretend I was sick. Ask to postpone it, or reschedule. Beg my doctor to forgo the blood work—I'd do the physical, I didn't care about that. My sugar was always kept in great control, I'd argue, asking why I needed to get lab work done. It wasn't like I was high all the time. He didn't buy it, though, and said that he still wanted to make sure my liver wasn't damaged, or anything else. The dragon's fire might scorch my insides, and without yearly blood work we wouldn't catch the damage until it was too late.

I walked with my father down the spiral staircase and watched as he handed the paperwork to the technician at the registration bay. She put a bracelet on my wrist like I was a prisoner: name, date of birth, treating physician. We continued down the hall, past the framed photos of aquatic life and starfish hanging on the bleak brown walls. The flat screen TV in the waiting room played Disney or Nickelodeon as it usually did, mounted below a sparkling painting of a fairy tale town. The aquarium bubbled and the small fish swam around inside, oblivious to any world but their own. I wished that I could join them, share in their blissful contentedness, only worried about what pirate ship to hide in and when the next round of flaky fish food would disturb the top of the water. Their scales glittered and flashed, red, blue, green, orange, darting in and out of the dilapidated castle and through the cascade of bubbles spewing from a rock half-submerged in sand-colored pebbles. I folded my hands in my lap as I sat, my feet barely touching the ground. A bookshelf rested against one wall, the volumes inside it piled rather than stacked. Though an avid reader, I didn't care to peruse the titles, my palms sweating, each moment bringing me closer to my execution.

A voice suddenly called out, like the hangman's, "Anthony!" We made eye contact. "You can come in now. This room right here," the nurse pointed. My dad came with me and sat in the chair while I sat on his lap, wedged in a corner. Vials lined the counter to our left, some empty, some filled with a dark red liquid. I looked away. Posters plastered the wall, all of smiling, happy cartoons.

"All set, Anthony?" said the nurse with a colorful lab coat, snapping on a pair of gloves.

I shook my head.

She chuckled. "Right arm or left?"

The platform on the chair was attached to the left side, and that's where the nurse sat too. And I was righty, so I didn't want that arm to be out of commission (because, of course, I wouldn't be able to use my arm for at least a day afterward, I reasoned, as my wound healed).

Thinking I was smarter than the dragon, I lifted my left arm.

I realized, that day, what a mistake I had made.

"Okay then," she said quietly. She picked up an acrid smelling strip of rubber and tied it around my bicep. It slapped against my skin, the loose ends of the knot dangling. I turned away.

"Make a fist, honey," she said.

I didn't.

I couldn't.

I squeezed my eyes shut.

"He doesn't do that," my dad said, coming to my rescue. "Just leave your arm loose," he said to me, trying to help me relax and explain how the needle is so small it passes right through the molecules. He couldn't have been more wrong, but I'm grateful that he at least did his best to calm me down.

The needle clicked. The dragon growled louder.

She pressed the soft skin on the inside of my elbow, searching for a vein, her neoprene gloves cold and slimy. A few moments went by. I didn't feel anything. Could she have done it already?

The steel bit into my flesh. I winced. At least it would be over soon now. The muscles in my neck ached from turning my head away.

A few more seconds went by, and she pulled the needle out. "Done already?" I asked. Quicker than usual. I even ventured a look at my arm.

I cried as she jabbed my elbow a second time, and the dragon roared.

"Sorry hon, I couldn't get a vein the first time."

I swallowed the apple in my throat and fought back tears, biting back the scream that roiled in my gut as she dug around in my elbow, searching for a vein. *Now it will be over soon*, I thought to myself, my toes curling in my shoes.

Again, she pulled it out. I didn't look. Good thing, because it ripped into my skin a third time.

"Just can't seem to get one," she mumbled.

When it came out, still without any blood in the vial, my dad intervened. "You're done," he said.

"But I didn't get—"

"You're done."

She shrugged, put a cotton ball and Band-Aid on my arm, and we left, my eyes puffy. (I probably screamed and cried a lot more than I'm letting on here, but I can't look like too much of a baby...). When I got over the shock (a few days later) I looked at my left elbow and realized that I didn't have a vein there. Sure, I had a small one, a barely visible blue line running down my arm, but that couldn't be big enough for a needle. I studied my right arm and noticed a big, thick vein practically bulging out at my elbow crease. From that day on, I've always had blood drawn from my right arm, and while I certainly don't enjoy it, I'd like to think I'm at least somewhat more composed as an adult than I was at eight. And I've never had a similar experience to what I endured that day.

I told myself as we walked out that at least I wouldn't have to go back for another year. A bit of a reprieve. But I worried about what Dr. Starkman would say, if he would make me give blood the next time I went for my quarterly appointment because they didn't get it this time. I knew what I'd say. "You had your chance, and you blew it. You're not jabbing me again until next year." I didn't know, though, if my dad would say the same thing. He usually was a great ally, but sometimes he couldn't understand. He just didn't know what I went through, not only with my yearly physical but every day I had to fight the dragon, taking shots and pricking my finger just to survive. I needed someone who knew what it felt like. Who does know, though? I wondered as we walked away from that dreadful room.

As a treat after my ordeal with the blood lab, my dad took me to the hospital gift shop. The shelves gleamed with sparkling toys and knick knacks, and I pattered along the floor from one aisle to the next. I held the stuffed animals, squeezing them in my hands—though I couldn't squeeze my left hand too much while I was recovering. Their soft fur melted between my fingers, and they looked at me with bright, black beady eyes. They didn't mind me hugging them tightly; they loved it as much as I did. I wanted them all, but my dad shook his head. "Find one you really like."

I put down the purple octopus that had wrapped its tentacles around my arms. He wouldn't have been very good against the dragon. "Sorry, Mr. Octopus," I said. "I can't get you today." I kept looking.

Could a cat fight the dragon? No, I reasoned. Could Kermit the frog fight the dragon? No, he might get too scared. Could a fish? Might swim away.

"Hmmm," I sighed. I considered a black dog when finally I saw him. He sat on the shelf alone, his plush feet hanging over the edge. Beige corduroy overalls, the same color as his fur, covered his knees to his belly, with two straps over his shoulders. A white t-shirt bore the Juvenile Diabetes Research Foundation's Walk to Cure Diabetes logo, four sneakers frozen mid-stride—yellow, blue, pink and red. A triangular face came to a point at his black nose, and a thin thread mouth smiled perpetually. Fur nearly obscured his dark glassy eyes, but I brushed it away. His eyes matched my hair; my eyes matched his fur.

I picked him up and looked more closely at his hands, feeling the scarlet heart-shaped patches. A metal bracelet circled his right wrist with a snake wrapped around a staff. *Medic Alert* it read. With the bear tucked under my arm, I went to my dad. "I found him," I said. I found my ally.

I asked the bear during the car ride home if he had had diabetes long.

He nodded.

"Since you were a kid?" I asked.

Nodded again.

"And you have to take insulin and get your fingers pricked every day?"

Another nod. He pointed to the red patches sewn onto his hands, the green patch on his stomach, the blue and orange patches on his thighs.

I smiled. "Well I do too, so you don't have to do it alone anymore." I held his hand tightly. He never said much, but that didn't bother me.

That night, when I had to take my insulin shot for dinner, I made sure my father gave Rufus his injection too. I pulled up Rufus's overalls. "You can get it here, like me," I said. "Now don't be afraid, it really doesn't hurt that badly. It will be real quick, one, two, three. Ready?" I asked. He nodded. I turned to my dad. "He's ready."

The needle pricked him, and he didn't even blink. I grinned. "I knew you'd be great," I told him after my dad left.

A "Normal" Day

I woke up to a flurry of white outside my window, the flakes falling thick and strong. Rufus was nestled in my armpit. Somehow he had managed to wedge himself in there during the course of my nocturnal flailing. My clock glared 8:30 AM in bright scarlet numbers. If my dad doesn't come wake me by 8:40, then there's a chance, I thought. I snuggled back under the blankets and pushed my head against my pillow, warding off the cold morning and the inevitable moment when I'd have to leave the warmth of the bed and brave the day.

8:33 came, inching slowly towards a snow day. Then 8:37. I said a quick prayer. My dad never waits this long to come wake me up if there's school.

At 8:39, the gleeful squeal of the hinges crushed my hopes. I refused to look, believing that, maybe, it was just my imagination, just a dream. Then my dad sang his morning jingle. "Time to get up, time to get up, time to get up in the morning!" Worse than an alarm clock buzzer.

"No school?" I asked from under the blankets.

"Nope."

"Really?" I cried, springing from the bed.

"Yup."

I studied his face more closely, watching the minute twitch at the corner of his mouth. I scowled. "You're just kidding."

"Yeah," he admitted sheepishly with a chuckle. "Come on, get dressed so you can eat breakfast."

"Aren't you going to check me?" I asked as he skipped steps two and three of my usual morning routine: 1) Wake up. 2) Dad checks blood sugar. 3) Dad gives insulin shot. 4) Get out of bed. 5) Get dressed. 6) Go downstairs. 7) Have breakfast. 8) Suffer through school.

"I checked when you were still sleeping and you were a little high so I gave you your shot already."

I rubbed my buttocks. I hadn't even felt anything. "So I can eat breakfast this morning like a normal kid?" I said smiling. No finger prick. No needle. I could get used to this experience of what it must be like for other kids to start their days, the kids who didn't have diabetes.

My dad looked at me with a frown. He put a hand on my shoulder and squeezed it. "AJ, you *are* a normal kid."

"I know that," I drawled. "I just mean I don't have to take a shot before I eat this morning. Like my friends." Seriously. Sometimes he was more sensitive about my diabetes than I was.

"Yes. But you are normal. As normal as any other kid. Everyone has something. Some kids have trouble learning. Some kids get sick a lot, some need glasses or can't hear very well. Some have diabetes. No one is perfect, and you're just as normal as everyone else."

"I know." I hugged Rufus and asked my dad if he got his shot already too. He did, so I quickly dressed, hurried downstairs, and ate my Cocoa Krispies not like a *normal* kid, but like a *non-diabetic* kid. And, despite the wintery flurries, I went to school with all the other normal kids of Salem Drive Elementary.

*****

I knew I was normal—I know I am now. But as diabetics, especially as children growing up with diabetes or diagnosed with it at a young age, we sometimes need a friend who experiences what we experience, who goes through the pains of having diabetes right alongside us. Sometimes, that friend is another person who has diabetes too. Maybe it's a brother or sister, a father or mother who also wrestles the dragon. But for those like myself who didn't know anyone else battling the beast, Rufus the bear was a great companion.

Sharon Kellaher tells of Rufus's origin for *Diabetes*

Health in an article published June 1, 1999. "Rufus...is full of love," she says, "but was born out of anger." Carol Cramer, the Illinois mother who created the first Rufus bear, says in an interview, "I was angry because my son [Brian] had to take on such a strong sense of bravery. He had to be even [braver] than me." Brian was three years old when the dragon first attacked him. We are brave, as Brian was, to battle the dragon as children. Yet even the bravest among us need allies. Rufus was mine. Facing the dragon alone can be a challenging ordeal. Its fire is hot, its talons sharp, and its fangs ruthless. But, Kellaher continues, "Rufus helped Brian to not feel alone or different...[He] helped to let Brian know that a child with diabetes is no more or less lovable a child. There are no labels. You are who you are because that's who you were created to be."

The dragon chose us because we are strong, because we make formidable opponents. We do not give up, we do not surrender. When the fight seems overwhelming, when we feel that we cannot go on, we look to our allies—our Rufuses—and wait for their nod, a nod that encourages us, supports us, sustains us. With a friend who fights the dragon with us, we continue the battle until we win; we never let the dragon defeat us, no matter how long it takes. Every day we fight and continue to fight, even if it lasts the rest of our lives.

We do not give up. We do not give in. We do not let the dragon win.

A Circus Charm

During the years after I found Rufus, my family had a tradition of going each summer to the Ringling Brothers and Barnum and Bailey Circus (which I've learned, to my great disappointment, has since performed its final show and closed its doors—or tents, I should say). I'd go with my dad, and some of my cousins, aunts and uncles. The circus offered the adventure of a lifetime to an imaginative ten-year-old, the pungent odor of animals wafting from the arena even into the parking lot. I bounced in the seat of the car as we pulled in, a Park Police Officer in a crisp blue uniform directing my dad where to park. I scanned the passing cars for my cousins' black Suburban or my uncle's beige Odyssey.

"There!" I exclaimed. I saw a black SUV. But it wasn't theirs. It didn't have the soccer ball bumper sticker that branded their vehicle. "Dad, call them," I insisted. He just shook his head as he parked. We got out, and he took the blue canvas duffel bag that contained my supplies should the dragon rear its head alongside the elephants and tigers. Juice boxes. Glucometer. Snacks. Insulin vials and syringes in an insulated case, and a bottle of water. A crowd milled in front of the entrance, pushing forward to get in through the glass doors, funneled by the brown bricks of the arena. I popped up on my toes, pressing into the people to find my cousins. "Where did they say they'd meet us?" I asked.

"They didn't. Don't worry, we'll find them."

We purchased our tickets, slipped past the gateman, and waited for a familiar face. A clown on stilts wobbled towards us, white paint covering his face. Blue circles surrounded his eyes, and a huge red ball replaced his nose. An explosion of orange hair erupted from his head. Some smaller kids screamed as he walked closer to them, but I returned his high-five when he came past me. Can't blame him for being so odd looking.

One of my uncles finally appeared, accompanied by my younger cousin Joe. I immediately left my dad and went to my cousin, our adventure for the day already percolating in my head. I hugged my uncle, then, after getting quick permission from our parents, we darted away to explore the venue before the circus actually began.

Each hallway appeared as a castle corridor to us, every room a treasure trove. The video games in a back alley begged us to play them, yet we didn't have their required price. No matter. The dark dungeons of the bathrooms offered a surprise behind every stall, some more pleasant than others, and we sauntered about until the prescribed time. One o'clock approached, and Joe and I hurried toward our seats. But before we gave up our adventure, we took a quick circuit of the three rings, examining each in turn. Ropes hung above one, like a spider's silky web. Barrels waited in another ring, stacked one upon the other. In the last ring, a large box waited, covered in a cloth, a shroud that shielded the mysterious cabinet from prying eyes. I tugged on Joey's sleeve. "You see it?" I asked.

"I see it," he answered. I leaned on the crimson barricade that circled the box.

"You zere!" a man called in a pitch black suit. "Away from zee box!" His angry mustache quivered as he pointed at us.

We scurried up to our seats before the casket's hidden danger could break free and devour us. Maybe a ruthless dragon waited inside.

Just as the lights dimmed and the Ring Leader took center stage, my other uncle and his trail of five kids filed into the empty seats beside us. Just in time.

"*Ladies and gentlemen,*" the announcer's voice boomed, "*welcome to the Ringling Brothers and Barnum and Bailey circus!*" A chorus of cheers and roaring applause answered him. He flipped the microphone cord dramatically, encouraging the crowd. *"A circus,"* he continued, *"that will amaze you with feats of aerial acrobatics beyond your wildest dreams."* More cheers. *"That will terrify you with a terrifically tall tiger."* My ears started to hurt. *"And finally astound you with a beast you've never seen before. A creature that cowers in the corners of the world, a monster you know only in myth and legend."* I looked to the box as my heart pounded and the reverberations in the arena nearly collapsed the roof. *"But without further ado, may I introduce the Ryma, a family of aerial acrobats from Romania!"* Boom. Cheer. Clap. Applaud. Let the act commence.

The music blasted from overhead speakers, pulsing through my bones and sending ripples down my spine. I bobbed my head to the familiar *Pirates of the Caribbean* theme song as the Ryma flipped, spun, jumped, trapezed, traipsed, tight walked, and contorted their bodies into impossible forms. Mikel, a sturdy young man wearing a sparkling white jump suit much too tight for his pecs, vaulted off the swinging bar, flipped three times backward, caught another bar, flipped again and landed on the small platform a hundred feet above the safety net.

"They should do that without a net under them," Rich said, my elder cousin by three years with whom I'd go on alien hunting adventures. (I'm serious. We even kept journals of our missions and concocted a complete codification system. We even found a partially melted golf-ball-sized green rubber ball in the shape of a monstrous head in the forest behind his house when we went exploring one day. We were convinced that it was dropped by a UFO after some experiment went wrong. But that's another story...)

"That'd really be a good trick."

Perhaps they heard him, because as Trima, a middle-aged acrobat bulkier than Mikel, prepared for her stunt, the Ring Leader announced, *"Ladies and gentlemen, observe the crew as Trima prepares for her jump. See them remove—yes remove—the safety netting that protects the performers."* Sure enough, the stage hands rolled up the tight, black, nearly invisible net as Trima climbed the ladder to the trapeze. I couldn't see, but I'm sure a bead of sweat popped up on her brow. The spotlight glared in her face. That's got to be hot. She gripped the wooden bar and tested the taut ropes before looking up. She raised her hand to the audience and leapt from the platform as though from a diving board, soaring through the air. She released the bar and flipped toward the next trapeze, rotating, spinning, falling. An outstretched arm reached for the bar, grasped at it, cried for it, pleaded for it.

A second passed. She spun.

Another second. She straightened.

Rich shoved a handful of popcorn in his mouth, and I looked at the bag hungrily.

Turning to my dad, I asked him if I could have some popcorn. I had to feed the dragon.

He handed me a weapon from the arsenal: my glucose monitor. "Test your sugar first." I didn't want to miss any of Trima's routine. But I also wanted popcorn. I hurriedly tore the alcohol, put the strip in the meter, changed the lancet, pricked my finger, let the test strip drink up the drop of blood, and pressed a cotton ball onto my wound. I balanced the monitor carefully on the armrest of my seat as I crushed all the other debris and shoved it in a side compartment of the Jeep bag.

Trima flailed for the bar.

A second in the air, reaching for it.

Her second expired, and she caught the bar with a grip of iron.

86 mg/dl, the meter beeped thirty seconds later.

"Ok," Dad said when I showed him. "That can be your snack."

The salty, buttery, airy kernels soiled my fingers as I scooped a handful from the striped bag my cousins shared. Now I could enjoy the next act in style.

I plucked each kernel delicately from my hand and put them on my tongue, preserving them, savoring them, chewing and sucking on them slowly with some water to wash it down.

A fearsome *roar* came from the second ring as the Ring Leader announced the next act. "*Though Redskin the tiger is no man-eater,*" he began, "*do not think him any less terrible! He has tasted meat, and hungers for it.*" The tamer in the ring dangled a lure at the end of a pole, taunting Redskin with it. The tiger snapped at it, though he never left the overturned barrel atop which he sat. His white fangs gleamed in the sharp light. The tamer, dressed in a sequin-studded black and orange body suit, twirled the lure, tossed it toward the tiger, and Redskin snatched at it with his gaping jaws.

The tiger pranced from barrel to barrel, standing on some, sitting on others. A chain link fence rose around him. The crew brought a hoop to the center of the ring. Once erected, it rose nearly as tall as the tiger's master, and reached a yard in diameter. "That'll be pretty impressive," whispered Joe, "if that big tiger gets through that."

"Yeah, he's gotta be a full-grown male," I said. "At least five hundred pounds." I swallowed another popcorn.

The master cracked a whip, and Redskin sauntered over to the hoop, stepping on a barrel and waiting for his cue. He leaped through, landed nimbly on his feet, and circled back around, baring his teeth and growling at the master. The man cracked the whip, keeping Redskin at a distance, backing up, retreating. Redskin stretched his jaw, yawning or getting ready to eat, and lay lazily in the center of the ring.

"It seems as though our tiger as grown tired!" The Ring Leader commented. *"Perhaps we need to liven him up a bit!"* The crowd answered the Ring Leader's call, but did nothing to invigorate the tiger who licked a claw. *"No? Perhaps some of his brothers then!"* More tigers trotted into the ring, circling around Redskin. Platforms bordered the inner edge of the ring, and at the *crack* of the tamer's whip, each tiger ran to his allotted place and awaited further instruction. Redskin climbed onto his own stool in the center and raised a paw, teasing the tamer, swatting playfully.

The tigers came down, crawled over one another's backs, jumped over more barrels and through more hoops, roared and bared their teeth. The tamer pumped his arms and pounded his chest like Tarzan, king of the jungle, tamer of beasts. The tigers obeyed his command, and he ruled his pack marvelously. But did he ever battle the dragon? Has he wrestled the beast?

The tigers finally slunk out of the ring, back through a dark portal into their cages. Then came the clowns, the magicians, the performers who could strip an entire outfit and replace it with something new in five seconds flat.

"Ladies and gentlemen," the Ring Leader finally rumbled in his baritone. "Prepare yourselves for our ultimate act. A sight that will amaze you, terrify you, astound you. A creature you know in fairy tale and legend is about to come alive before your very eyes."

I stared at the box in the ring. Did it shudder, or was that my imagination? The Ring Leader pulled the cloth away, and it drifted to the floor in a billowing heap.

A walking vendor approached our aisle, hawking his sweets, goodies, and treats. Fluffy heaps of pink and blue cotton candy lined his tray, along with richly colored snow cones, bags of candy, and pretzels. I looked longingly at the food, distracted for a moment from the Ring Leader's introduction. Cotton candy. I wondered what it tasted like. It enticed me as the lure enticed Redskin. Joe asked his dad for a blue cotton candy. Rich got a pink one. Molly got a purple one. Dad got a pretzel. I salivated and got my own spit. The dragon started to roar inside me, clawing at my belly not with hunger but with jealousy. I watched as my family enjoyed their treats, as my dad indulged in the soft, doughy treat.

"Can I have a piece?" I asked. I could have one piece. "What about cotton candy?" I pleaded as wisps flew from my cousins' spun treats faster than the acrobats. I clenched my fist. No. I couldn't have any of that. I already had my snack. And cotton candy was off limits. When I asked for a snow cone, I got a cup of plain ice.

"Ladies and gentlemen," the Ring Leader continued, "I present to you Ringling Brothers and Barnum and Bailey's DRAGON!"

I probably should've been more amazed, although part of me knew it was just a hoax. Performers in costumes and animatronics. But I had my own dragon roaring inside me as the envy stirred in my gut. Why couldn't I be like my cousins? Why couldn't I eat cotton candy like them? Why did I have to be the diabetic? Why couldn't I be like everyone else…?

I'd like to say that I didn't begrudge my family their enjoyment, but it would be a lie. I couldn't eat any of those delicious treats, and no one likes to be alone in their suffering. Rufus understood, but he stayed home that day, slowly forgotten in the mind of a sixth-grader.

Cotton candy taunted me when I looked upon it at the circus and on the boardwalk. Rainbow snow cones teased me at every Disney on Ice show. But it taunts every child, and perhaps unfairly so. For they aren't shielded against its power as I was. The dragon, in forcing me to fight it, actually strengthened me and gave me the courage to say "No" to unhealthy food. The shield I used against the dragon's fire became the same shield I used against the poison of sugar. Though the dragon certainly hurt me emotionally, I've since learned that it was in fact a great benefit to my physical health. Despite the torture of diabetes and the dietary restrictions it required, I must thank diabetes for forcing me to eat the way every healthy, non-diabetic child should. Although I suppose a treat every now and then for a rare occasion doesn't hurt.

*****

As I got older, I did try cotton candy—I might have been sixteen or seventeen. When I finally tasted it, instead of discovering the long-anticipated grail of carney food, I encountered a rather lackluster cloud of sickly-sweet air. I couldn't swallow more than a few mouthfuls even as the crystals dissolved on my tongue, and I realized that cotton candy wasn't anything special. And with the advent of new insulin regimens such as basal/bolus[1] and the insulin pump,

---

[1] Basal/bolus insulin therapy requires multiple injections of insulin each day. Bolus insulin injections are taken at each meal or whenever a diabetic has to correct for a high blood sugar, while the basal insulin dosage is taken once per day to establish a "baseline" to regulate the sugars naturally produced by the liver.

the abstinence from sugary treats may now exist only in the past for type I diabetics (though it still acutely affects those with type II). However, sugar can still be a deadly enemy for anyone who wrestles the dragon. It can feed the beast and fuel its fire if consumed recklessly or wantonly. The dragon savors the sugar of cotton candy, snow cones, and sodas, while fruits, juices, and vegetables can help douse its fire. Do not feed the dragon, either with bitterness or with temptation. It attacked me at the circus, and in that moment I let jealousy consume me. I lost that fight because I hated myself for being a diabetic. But I have since used that defeat to turn my weakness into a strength, understanding that, to beat the dragon, I cannot surrender to every impulse and desire—and I shouldn't begrudge my friends or family their enjoyment. And so even in winning a battle, the dragon did not win the war.

Snowball Fight

The snow fell soft and cold that night in deep long drifts. I swam through it with my friend Jesse from up the block, bundled in my insulated one-piece snow suit. We made forts, we tried to make a snowman, we threw snowballs at each other for a while as the persistent flakes landed on our noses.

"What did you think about that vocab test?" Jesse asked as we lay on our backs, cushioned by a bed of snow.

"Easy," I said. "How about you?"

"Not bad." My backyard seemed vast when layered in white, the trees of the surrounding forest ghostly and skeletal, framed by the dense gray sky.

"What should we do now?" I stuck my tongue out, collecting as many flakes as I could.

"I don't know. What do you want to do?"

My neighbors had a playset with swings and a slide and a tower with a canopy for their younger kids. "We could sneak over there," I suggested.

"Out in the open? Risky. I like it." He pulled his wool cap tighter.

We skirted the forest's edge, snuck up the tower, hid

there as the snow kept falling. I peered toward the house, examining the windows with lights on. Was anyone looking out? Did they see us? What would they do if they saw us on their playset? Was that a shadow that just passed over one? A silhouette? I ducked behind the wooden railing.

"What now?" Jesse asked, crawling halfway into the tunnel slide.

"This can be our fort." I started amassing snowballs in case the imaginary troopers stormed our newfound castle.

We pretended to defend it for a while. Then Jesse said, "Let's go take a real castle."

"What?"

He jerked his head toward the house.

"What are you talking about?"

"This isn't a real fort. Too exposed. Come on." He slid down the slide, landing on his butt. I climbed down the rope ladder.

"Jesse, what are you doing?" I whispered. "We're leaving tracks."

"Whoops. The snow will cover them. It doesn't look like it's going to stop anytime soon."

He still backtracked to the edge of the woods and dragged me back to the edge of my yard. We went to the other side of my house and hugged it all the way around until we made it back to the side adjacent to my neighbor's house. They had a sliding glass door that led to their basement, and a glow of soft light spilled out past the curtains onto a small patio. Jesse dove for the brick wall and lay flat against it.

"Jesse, what are you doing?" I whisper-shouted. Suddenly my hands felt sweaty, and the tell-tale lull of fatigue nagged at my body. And I didn't have juice nearby.

Jesse rolled a ball of snow in his hands and waved me over.

"Are you stupid?" I seethed, the dragon's anger taking over. It wanted food, and I wasn't feeding it.

Jesse hurled the snowball at the glass door, leaving a splatter of ice. His face twisted in a giggle, and my blood started to boil. "You're going to get us in trouble," I mouthed, a fresh wave of anxiety washing over me, amplified by the dragon's poison.

"Do it." He handed me a snowball.

Half-delirious, mad at Jesse, mad at the dragon, I threw it and ran, pressing my back against the side of their house. I heard the door open, and our neighbor stuck her head out. "Hey, stop that!" she yelled. "I know it's you."

Did she know who it was? Who else could it be? The dragon laughed at me, sweat soaking my undershirt, my head spinning.

I ran to my front yard, Jesse following. "You are such an idiot," I said. "You always come up with the dumbest ideas. If I get in trouble, I'm blaming you." It was the dragon talking. But Jesse didn't know that.

"What's your problem, AJ?"

"I don't have a problem. You're the problem."

"Okay." He went home that night without saying goodbye.

I went inside, and my dad gave me orange juice, scolding me for not coming in sooner. "AJ, come on!" he said. "What if you passed out? What if I couldn't find you? You know better than that. As soon as you start feeling low, immediately come inside."

I stayed friends with Jesse, of course, but I never apologized. It wasn't my fault, after all; it was the dragon's fault. It was the dragon who made me irritable. It was the dragon who threw that snowball.

Lying Low in School

Snack time was one of my favorite activities at Salem Drive Elementary School, even though it marked me as different. The other kids didn't get to enjoy it like I did, and I sometimes disliked the special attention. My classmates would always ask me to share my fruit Gushers. I really couldn't blame them. I completely understood the TV commercials where the kids would go crazy for those delicious, juice-filled gummies. Sometimes I slipped a few to my friends.

On one particular day, our fifth-grade teacher, Mrs. Duer, handed out a spelling test. My heart thudded against my chest. The black ink of the blank lines overwhelmed me. But I knew how to spell. I hoped I did. I had studied. *Drive. Light. Racecar. A lot. House. Ceiling.* The words spun around inside my memory. I wished the test had a word bank.

The letters started to jumble together. I *before* e *except after* c, I kept repeating to myself. *But what about the exceptions? Space between* a *and* lot. *Or was it no space?* I checked the point on my pencil, prodding the soft pad of my index finger with it. I worried it might break, scraped a fingernail against the yellow wood. The blank chalkboard offered no assistance as we took our test, the green surface wide and empty. I drummed my fingers against the hollow shelf of my desk, my books stacked safely inside, closed and secure.

The tip of my pencil scratched at the paper. Mrs. Duer called out a word. And another. And another. My mind got fuzzy. Why couldn't I remember these words? The soft gray lines of my answers taunted me. I tapped my foot. I slapped the pencil's eraser against the desk. A sense of anxiety boiled inside me. Why was I so nervous? Why was I sweating?

I glanced at my classmates. Frowns twisted some mouths; smiles curled some lips; one boy stared out the window.

I rubbed out a letter with the dirty eraser, smudging it, nearly ripping the page. My clammy palms moistened the paper. *D-r-a-w-i-n-*

Then I felt it. The dragon inside me. It started with a low growl, a light wisp of smoke steaming from its flaring nostrils. I went on. Maybe I'd get through the test without angering it any further.

-g.

It shifted inside me, unfurling its wings and stretching its claws. I felt a battle brewing.

Mrs. Duer called out the next word, but I didn't hear. I raised my hand.

"Yes, AJ?" she asked, looking at me with gentle eyes.

"Could you say that word again?"

"Sure. *Driveway.*" Her voice jogged my memory, and I quickly jotted down my answer.

But the dragon wouldn't stand for that. My palms grew clammier, and beads of sweat dripped down my leg. My shirt clung to my stomach.

I looked at the clock. Forty minutes until lunch.

Ten more words to go.

If I went to the nurse for juice, I'd miss the rest of the test.

Quiet you, I told the beast. I'll feed you soon enough.

The paper in front of me suddenly blurred. I blinked and squinted at the white sheet, moving my head back and forth. *Please hurry up, Mrs. Duer.* I didn't want to leave. I didn't want to be the kid who had to get up in front of the whole class while everyone else sat quietly taking their test.

But the dragon called to me, howled at me, slashed at me. It wanted to fight. The letters continued to jumble in my head even worse than before. *If I go on, I might as well write Chinese for these last few words. If they're any sort of difficult, the dragon will distract me too much to get them right.*

The next word. "*Peninsula.*"

Great. Does it have one n or two? One l or two? Is the first vowel an i or an e?

I gave it my best guess.

"Competitor."

More guesswork.

"Finished."

Finally! Oh wait, that's a word. I think I know this one, at least.

The end eventually did come, three words later. Mrs. Duer collected our tests and stacked them in a neat pile on her desk, posters hanging from the front of the gray table and a porcelain apple sitting enticingly on top of it. The dragon roared louder, fire spewing from its mouth. Its breath confused me, fogging my mind, making my head heavy.

"Ok," Mrs. Duer said, "we'll go over the words for next week's unit in the half hour we have before lunch time."

I couldn't wait any longer. I had to fight the dragon now.

I got up from my seat, the navy blue plastic heavy in my hands as I pushed it back, scraping the linoleum floor. Each tile occupied one square foot. I'm not sure why I noticed such trivial things when my blood sugar dropped. The eyes of the other students snapped toward me. Mrs. Duer paused, her face not angry but concerned.

I walked up to the front of the class, through the labyrinth of other desks, each with an inquisitive boy or girl sitting behind it, wondering why I had to get up and go to the teacher. A scarlet blush drowned out the freckles on my cheeks, and I floated in a whirlwind of imagined attention and curiosity. The maze took me forever to traverse, but I succeeded and stood in front of the teacher.

"I feel low, can I go to the nurse?" I blurted out.

"Of course!" Mrs. Duer said. "Do you need someone to go with you?"

I shook my head. The dragon flailed, restless and agitated.

"Okay then, go, go!" she said, herding me to the door with a mother's touch. I rushed out of the room, trying to ignore my thoughts of the other students' laughter at the sick boy having to go to the nurse. They probably didn't laugh. In fact, I'm sure they didn't. But at the time, a thousand screams of jeering classmates berated my ears, cheerleaders for the dragon.

I waved to Mrs. Walsh, the main office secretary, then slipped into Mrs. Busby's domain, the safe haven of Salem Drive's nurse.

"Feeling a little low?" she asked as I walked in, her name embroidered in cursive script on her white coat.

"Yeah." I got my shoe box from its space on her shelf. The people printed on the box ran on tread climbers, some played basketball or tennis, some ran a marathon; others lifted weights, rode a bicycle, or boxed. *Boxing on a shoe box*, I tittered, tickled even as the dragon breathed fire at me.

Mrs. Busby came and watched over my shoulder. I wiped my finger with alcohol, dabbed it with a cotton ball, inserted the test strip into the meter, waiting for it to warm up. I pricked my finger, a red drop of blood emerging. I held it to the hungry green test strip, and the meter slurped it up, as hungry for my blood as the dragon for food.

30 the meter read. *29, 28, 27...*

Come on, I urged, willing it to go faster. It didn't.

15, 14, 13...

I could already taste the berry-flavored Juicy Juice box that waited in Mrs. Busby's fridge, a fresh pack of eight with the plastic still sealing them.

3, 2, 1.

41 mg/dl.

I ran to the fridge, barely taking the time to remove the test strip from the meter, and whipped out the eight-pack of juice boxes. My fingernail bit into the plastic wrapping, slicing it open. The juice box came out, the straw pierced the foil seal, and the sweet juice washed down my throat, settling in my stomach as a rush of ecstasy shot through me. The dragon got what it wanted, but such a meager offering did not fully appease it. The growls continued, even with the fire dampened. That's when the saltine crackers came out, a beautiful cardboard box with a lovely picture of a perfect cracker on the front. I slipped my finger under the flap, popped the tab from the slot. I wrenched three crackers from the sleeve and crunched them, savoring each bite, letting the salty flakes settle on my tongue and dissolve before swallowing. I wanted more. I wanted the entire sleeve. The entire box. Just eat and eat and eat and not stop eating until my stomach exploded. The dragon grumbled for it, demanding it. But Mrs. Busby wouldn't give me any more. I just had to wait until lunch.

I sat on the blue beds in Mrs. Busby's office. Then I bounced to a seat by her desk. I offered my assistance when other students came in with their ailments and pains. To pass the time, Mrs. Busby and I even had our own sword fight with sleeves of paper cups still in their plastic shrouds. I won—my experience with the dragon gave me an unfair advantage. Slowly, the dragon's roars went away, and it slunk back into the cave where it'd wait until the next fight.

For now, I had satisfied it; I had fed the beast and emerged unscathed.

Ten minutes until lunch. Soon, the other diabetic student came in. Dylan was a few grades below me. When he checked his sugar, I checked mine again to make sure the dragon had completely calmed. *94 mg/dl.*

"Okay, AJ, looks good," Mrs. Busby said. "You can go to lunch now."

I returned my box to the shelf. Throughout my years of elementary and middle school, I always disliked having to leave class because I started to feel my blood sugar going low. I'd prefer to wait until lunch, when my teachers knew I had to go to the nurse anyway to check my blood sugar, but sometimes I just couldn't wait. Sometimes it would be dangerous to wait. The dragon's roar is not easily ignored, and can bring disastrous consequences if it is. That's why, as we wrestle the dragon, we must not let our own personal feelings, reservations, or discomfort get in the way of our fight. If we do, defeat—or worse—is sure to follow.

In the sixth or seventh grade, I discovered a new alternative to going to the nurse's office every time I felt the dragon start to growl: Glucose tablets and a box of raisins. My first set of tablets came in foil wrapping, with a plastic shell. The white tablets had an orange flavor, and had the letters *BD* stamped into them. I started keeping a pair of them in my pocket along with a small red box of Sunmaid raisins. When the dragon began to growl, I took one out, popped it into my mouth, let it dissolve as I chewed it, and so satisfied the dragon long enough to last until lunch. Sometimes I'd have the raisins too, but if I didn't eat them soon, the box would get all mushy and sometimes the raisins would fall out and soil my pocket. I stopped carrying those after a while.

But this new method brought with it its own complications. What if someone saw me popping white tablets in class? Would they think it was drugs? I tried to be as discreet as possible whenever I had to chew one, but each crinkle of the foil made my face flush. During an assembly once, in ninth grade, I remember sitting in the front row. The dragon growled. I reached into my pocket as inconspicuously as I could, feeling for the bundle that would quiet the beast. I struggled to remove the rubber band that held them together, operating with only one hand. When I succeeded, I pressed the plastic case, pushing out the square tablet from the foil, and quickly slipped it into my mouth. I worried that the kid sitting next to me would see it, but in the end, quieting the dragon was more important than whatever anyone else might think.

An innovation soon helped to relieve some of my discomfort: a tube of round glucose tablets, these coming in flavors such as raspberry, apple, even coconut. The top popped off easily, and I could carry more than just two. For years, I kept a sleeve in my pocket wherever I went.

But sometimes, even glucose tablets can be inconvenient. I would go low during sports practices and games, when I used to play soccer and basketball for the township rec team. I had the luxury of having my dad as the coach, so I could always go to him for juice when I needed it. For parents who can't always be close by for their diabetic kids, I can imagine the stress of sending off a son or daughter and having to worry about the coach watching their child, hoping they know the warning signs of hypoglycemia and how to administer a glucagon shot should their child pass out. There are ways to prevent the dragon from attacking, though—having a snack before games and practices, or keeping Gatorade or juice nearby.

There were times when I would go low during recess at school, have to cut it short to go to the nurse's office. I would go low—and still do—in the middle of the night when my sweat turns the bed into a swimming pool. I've even gone low while writing this book… (like right now).

Unfortunately, low blood sugar is something we who

wrestle the dragon must contend with to maintain tight glycemic control, even though it can certainly dampen a good time. It has forced me out of the town pool while my friends got to stay and play; forced me to wait in the chair at the beach while my cousins played Frisbee or volleyball or tag. But I do love food, so if being a diabetic gives me an excuse to have a snack before running around and exercising, I guess I'll have to take the good with the bad.

Shots

(But Not the Kind You

Think)

The Blockbuster aisles enticed me, the thick plastic covers of VHS tapes covering the shelves. (For those of you who haven't even heard of Blockbuster, it used to be a widely popular video rental chain before the days of Netflix and online streaming. Imagine having to leave your house, get in a car, and drive somewhere every time you wanted to rent a movie. Then making sure you rewound the tape and got it back to the store before the due date. Like a library, but for movies. I know. The thought is terrifying. But for me (and perhaps for others as well), there is a certain nostalgia in those memories—a certain excitement that would always course through me when I perused the different aisles

[Drama, Romantic Comedy, Action, Kids] that I can never seem to find in clicking through the twenty-first-century equivalents, plodding through thousands of choices on a television screen.)

"What should we watch tonight?" I tugged on my mom's pocketbook. "Can we get a few?"

"Sure, as long as you think we'll get to watch them all before we have to bring them back."

I searched through the *Kids* aisle, checking the cartoon movies, looking for the Ninja Turtles—they were one of my favorites—while my mom looked at the dramas. The boring adult stuff. (We went to one Blockbuster, once, that had a curtain shielding an "adult" area. I wasn't supposed to go in there, but when no one was looking I slipped through the dangling beads. I almost brought out one of the more interesting videos—one with a rather revealing cover—and asked my mom if we could rent it, but I ultimately decided that it probably wouldn't be the best idea and snuck back out before anyone noticed.)

This Blockbuster didn't have such an elaborate pornographic section, and we both made our selections and stood in line at the checkout counter. My mouth started to water as we passed the ice cream cooler, and I couldn't help myself from sliding open the glass door and looking through the different treats, knowing I couldn't have any. But maybe, maybe there would be something sugar free, or something with just a little bit of sugar. Even though I knew it wouldn't be there, I looked. I felt the crisp plastic wrappers, the nutty toppings on a chocolate almond éclair, wishing I could sink my teeth into a perfectly round chocolate chip cookie Chipwich.

"Can I get one? Please?" I begged, proffering the ice cream sandwich to my mom like a sacrificial offering. The dragon writhed in my stomach, hissing and spraying its fire.

"How much sugar does it have?"

"Twenty-eight," I drawled, hoping that if I said it slowly enough she might not hear correctly.

"That's too much, AJ. You know that."

Yeah. I did know that. But, hey, I still had to try, right? I threw it back into the cooler when a small green container caught my eye. Something from Popsicle called Shots. I picked up the little cup-shaped thing, the cold cardboard leeching the warmth from my hand. I quickly searched for the nutrition facts label and...my eyes shot open. Could I really be reading this correctly? I looked again. And again. And a third time, blinking to make sure I wasn't missing something. I picked up another one to make sure it wasn't just a typo.

"Mom!" I shouted as she handed the clerk our videos. "Can I get this one?"

"What is it?" she asked, fishing through her pocketbook for her wallet.

"Shots. And it only has four grams of sugar!"

"Really? Only four? Let me see." She took it from my hand and studied the label. "Huh. Wow. Yeah, I guess you can have that." The cashier swiped it at the register, and the iconic *beep* sounded more gratifying to me than it ever had before. A smile blossomed across my face as I anticipated what it would be like to dump those lemon-lime ice balls into my mouth, savor them for a while before they melted and trickled down into my stomach.

I tore open the flap before we even left the store, and each mouthful was as good as I imagined it would be. The dragon shifted in my belly, unsure of how to react. I was eating sugar—pure sugar—but only four grams worth for this entire cup. It was almost too good to be true...

We popped in the movie at my mom's condo[1] while I finished off the last few Shots—I had to make them last, and stretched them out as long as I possibly could. My knuckles

---

[1] My parents divorced when I was fairly young (a few years after my diagnosis), which created a separate challenge of making sure both homes were fully stocked with diabetes supplies and requiring ongoing dialogue between my parents regarding my diabetes care

popped with the excitement of a diabetic kid who finally found an ice cream treat that he could eat. "I still can't believe this was only four grams," I said, looking at the nutrition label again, searching for the secret, the trick, the rub. "Four grams for….oh crap."

A spasm of fear shot through my legs, and my knees nearly buckled. I held out the green cup and told my mom to read the serving size. "One piece. Four grams per one piece."

"AJ," my mom said, suddenly nervous. "How many pieces were there?"

I said there must have been a hundred. They were little beads of ice. All packed in the cup.

"Oh my God, AJ." She gave me a whole needle's worth of insulin, her hands shaking. I winced when she stabbed my arm, and the dragon growled, laughing, cackling, realizing it got the best of me yet again. I knew it was too good to be true. I knew there had to be some catch. I knew there couldn't really be an ice cream I could eat.

She called the company the next day and wrote a scathing letter. Turns out, funny enough, that it *was* only four grams of sugar for the entire package. The label was just misleading. After her letter, though, Popsicle changed the wording. When I saw the Shots cup again a few months later, the nutrition facts said: Serving Size: 1 container. But it would still take a while for me to risk trying it again, just in case. It would take a while for me to get over the shock of having a dream come true pulled out from under me so instantaneously, even if it was just a case of misleading information. (Funny, how life has a habit of doing that to me, first with the Shots, then again with the Secret Service.) Hopefully, though, Popsicle will realize the danger of misrepresenting information on their labels and will be mindful in the future of how it might affect those who actually care about reading the nutrition facts.

PART II

❧❧❧❧ ✠ ✤ ✠ ❧❧❧❧

MATURING WITH THE DRAGON

Taking the Dragon by the

Horns

Every summer until my thirteenth birthday my mom would take me to Point Pleasant beach on the Jersey Shore. Often we'd go just for a day trip, but sometimes we'd stay for a week. One warm day, I told my mom spur of the moment that we should go to Point Pleasant. School had let out a few weeks earlier—I became an official seventh-grader!—and the golden sun warmed my face, encouraging my adventurous side.

Mom twisted her mouth, considering.

"Come on," I said, "please!"

"Ok, I guess we can go."

"Yes!" I rocketed upstairs to change into my bathing suit while Mom stocked my diabetes arsenal with juice boxes, an apple, banana, vials of insulin, and syringes (along with the ice pack to keep them cool in the days before insulin pens that can be left out at room temperature).

On the parkway, I rummaged through the glove compartment of my mom's pickup, browsing my stockpile of sugar free gum and candies. Trident, some sugar free licorice, a sleeve of Necco candy wafers that I loved to put on my tongue and press against the roof of my mouth until they cracked. I popped a piece of watermelon Bubblicious in my mouth and stuck my arm out the window, weaving it up and down through the air as the truck sliced down the highway. My fingers spread and caught the wind as it pushed against my hand.

A little silver car zipped in front of us, nearly hitting our front bumper. "What a nut!" I yelled. "Cut in front of her! Don't let her get away with that." How dare this selfish silver car delay our trip to the beach.

Mom looked at me strangely, an eyebrow raised. "That's a big word for you."

"What word? *Front*?"

"No, *confront*. You know what that means?"

"Confront? I didn't say confront. I said *cut in front of her*."

"Oh! I thought you said I should *confront* her."

"Well you could do that too."

The green parkway signs flashed by. Exit 130. 124. I started counting mile markers. Exit 100B. 100A. Finally, 98 appeared.

EXIT 98
EAST 138 34 TO INTERSTATE 195
Belmar Pt. Pleasant Trenton
EXIT 1 ¾ MILES

Soon. Soon I'd feel the sand between my toes. We pulled off the parkway and onto the familiar roads and streets that marked the path to Point Pleasant Beach. Over the drawbridge we went, the sweet, salty smell of the shore filling the truck, invigorating and refreshing. I peeked through the rows of houses trying to glimpse the boardwalk.

"Arcade first." I outlined my itinerary. "Then pizza at Little Mack's, then beach, then rides, then dinner!" I had the day all planned. "Maybe the aquarium too if there's time."

We found an open lot next to my favorite arcade. I hopped out, and Mom had to chase me up the ramp, through the maze of amusement rides, and into Jenkinson's on the boardwalk. The games glittered and winked at me, hungry for quarters. Prizes smiled from the shelves, goodies and trinkets that would only cost 100,000 tokens. I played for a while, depleting the small handful of coins I carried before pestering my mom for another twenty dollars. I think I got around five thousand points that day.

After I had redeemed the coupons and received a

voucher for use on a future prize, my stomach grumbled.
"Time for lunch." I headed towards the boardwalk and the
best pizza place in Point Pleasant. I eyed the rows of fresh
pizzas steaming on the counter behind the glass. So many to
choose from. "I'll have two plain," I told my mom. I always
got plain. And from all the excitement in the arcade, I had
worked up an appetite.

"Two?" she said. "You'll have to do some exercise on
the beach after."

"Don't I always?" I was hungry. I wanted two.

Large bay windows overlooked the beach, several
opened to welcome the breeze. I polished off the two slices
with a Diet Pepsi and savored the combination of smells
mixing in the air: fresh pizza and ocean air. I pulled on my
mom's sleeve. "Can I have another slice? I was only
seventy." Some sauce clung to my cheek, and I wiped it off.

"You'll have to do a lot of exercise just to work off what
you had already."

"But I'll play in the ocean and on the beach. Please. I'll
do jumping jacks."

She shook her head.

Slightly disgruntled, I collected the paper plates and
napkins and whisked off to the pearly white and yellow sand
of Point Pleasant Beach, passing the candy shop that

sometimes had sugar free taffy.

I ran to calm the dragon. I fought it in the sea and on the land until I won the battle. Drying off with a towel and rinsing my feet with the faucet on the steps near the boardwalk, I took a quick detour back to the truck to change out of my bathing suit and into more comfortable clothing. Grateful for the tinted windows, I stripped down to my birthday suit. A spot of fire flared on my cheeks as someone walked by. I froze and waited until she passed before pulling up my shorts, fastening my belt and slipping into my shirt.

Mom waited for me outside the car. "No time for the aquarium before dinner," she said, "but we can go on the boardwalk for a bit." I wondered if I'd get my favorite ice cream from Khors: a vanilla and orange sherbet twist. If I did, I'd have to take extra insulin for my dinner shot later.

I walked towards the aquarium anyway, hoping for a peek inside its gift shop. Interesting nautical trinkets always cluttered the shelves. We never reached the shop, though, stopping at a small fortune teller's cubby nestled between another arcade and the aquarium's entrance. A flurry of words above the door read, *To know thy future is to hold power in thine hands.*

The words drew me in, pulling me closer.

Mom asked, "Do you want your palm read?"

I put my hands in my pockets. "I don't believe in that crap. They just say really vague things that could apply to anyone."

Still, we went inside. A few other people sat in the small waiting area: an old woman with a light brown coat; a twenty-something-year-old with his girlfriend, his arm around her waist; a man reading a pamphlet taken from the antique wooden stand next to the leather couch. *Fortune's Favor for the Fortunate*, was the pamphlet's title. A large mirror hung on the wall, doubling everything in the room. The dim lighting pushed away the sunbeams trying to penetrate from outside, a thin haze of incense lingering in the air. Bright red cushions covered the armchairs, and I plopped into one. "Where is this lady?" I whispered to my mom. A portrait of the fortune teller stared at us from above the mirror, a mole on her cheek just below one of her dark eyes, her lips the color of strawberries, cobalt eye shadow giving her a ghostly look.

A heavy red curtain hid the rear chambers. I tapped my foot on the intricate carpeting. "If she doesn't come out soon…"

The drapes rustled. A woman peered out from behind them, resembling the portrait. The man reading the pamphlet set it down.

Her eyes met mine, and her lips curled in a smile. "You," she beckoned, her voice floating to me, carried on the wisps of smoke; foreign, European, exotic.

I rose, leaving my mother behind. She said, "I'll wait for you here."

I barely heard her as I brushed the curtain aside, entering the dark room heavy with mystery. A few candles burned in the corners. Could this lady really know my future? Her sequins jingled like glass as she gestured to a hard wooden stool, a plain table in front of me. She sat on the opposite side, looking into my eyes. I glanced at the whorls and grains of the tabletop, my fingers interlaced, resting in my lap.

"Give me your palm." Her soft words coiled around me.

I laid my right hand on the table, and she grasped it with her own warm, smooth fingers. A scarlet nail traced the lines on my palm, and a tingle shot up my arm, radiating even to my toes. Her delicate eyebrows scrunched as her eyes narrowed. "You will have long life," she said. "You will marry once and have a happy marriage." Ok, good so far. "Two children you will have. Two boys." Fair enough. Will the dragon live inside them too? "But there will be struggles." Here it comes. "A battle rages around you and within you. Long life is yours, but you will fight for it." Well I guess I already knew that. But will I have the dragon my entire life? Will someone discover a cure? Will another disease ally itself with the dragon against me?

I couldn't bring myself to ask these questions.

She smiled and pressed her fingers into the skin of my palm. "Good luck to you." A draft snuck through the curtains and the candles flickered.

We walked out into the waiting room, and my mom stood up. "How much?" she asked, taking out her wallet.

"For such a cute boy, ten dollars."

"Oh. Thank you," Mom said, handing over the bill. "Come on AJ, let's go get dinner."

I looked back at the lady. The man reading the pamphlet had left, and the room seemed a bit darker. "What'd she say?" mom asked.

"The usual. Two kids. Long, happy marriage."

For dinner, I said I wanted to go to my favorite rib place in Point Pleasant. Southern House, I think it was called. It burned down a few years later.

"Could've guessed that," mom laughed. Back to the car we went for my insulin, down the boardwalk and through the maze of amusement rides. The Crazy School Bus went round and round, the Roller Coaster climbed the hills and plummeted into the valleys, the Merry-Go-Round spun and spun, and the train ride tooted its whistle as it carried tourists through the park.

In the truck, my mom took out the small beige case from the insulated cooler pack. I consulted my log book, deciding how many units I should take, comparing dosages from past meals when I had eaten ribs. I wiped the top of the vial with alcohol, punctured the rubber cap with the syringe, injected the proper amount of air into the vial, drew back the plunger, back and forth until the black rubber aligned with the correct tick mark on the barrel of the syringe.

I pulled up the leg of my shorts, exposing the skin of my thigh, wiped the site with alcohol, waved my hand to dry it off, then gave the syringe to my mom.

I'd never given myself a shot before.

For months, Dr. Starkman had encouraged me to start giving myself my own injections, but the idea horrified me. How could I stab myself? I'd given Rufus his insulin before, that wasn't a problem. But stab myself? No thank you. Finger pricks I could do. Jabbing a needle into my body was a different story. Dr. Starkman suggested practicing on an orange, though I never really understood the theory behind that. An orange isn't me, it isn't flesh and bone, it doesn't *feel*. Sometimes, lying on my back on the couch at home, I'd anticipate the moment when my dad stuck the needle in my leg. Sometimes it hurt, sometimes it didn't. Sometimes the pain made me squeeze my eyes shut and wince, sometimes it felt like nothing more than a quick pinch—other times I didn't feel it at all. But which would it be? What if I injected myself and the pain made my hand flinch? What if the needle broke off inside me?

These questions haunted me, scared me, held me back from taking that next big leap. They kept me from taking the dragon by its horns, prevented me from severing my dependence on my parents. I could never stay long without them. I couldn't sleep over my friend's house or my cousin's without one of my parents there. What kind of knight could I be, battling a dragon when I couldn't even face my own fears?

Sitting in that truck in the parking lot of Point Pleasant, I considered these scenarios. My mom held the needle ready and asked where I wanted it. The silver tip glinted, and a drop of cloudy insulin leaked out, quivering before dropping onto the center console. *The console*, I seethed. *That's the problem. She can't reach over the console.* I swallowed. "Just give me the needle," I said quickly. I took it. Pinched my thigh. And stabbed my leg.

The dragon growled as the antidote seeped into my blood stream. I had done it. I lanced the dragon. Finally, I understood that to pierce the dragon's heart, I needed to pierce myself. He lived inside me and would devour me from within if I didn't fight back. My parents wouldn't always be there to hold my sword for me. So I took the first step that day in Point Pleasant. Out of necessity, in the interest of practicality, I gave myself my first injection.

We went to the restaurant and had a great dinner: ribs smothered in barbeque sauce, mashed potatoes, corn bread, rice, and even some of my mom's lobster. With our bellies full, we hopped back on the Parkway North. I flexed my sword arm, remembering the feeling of the syringe as I pushed the plunger down. I can fight the dragon myself, now that I know how to hold the sword. And in holding the sword, I held my future.

My parents never gave me another shot again.

Public Injection No. 1

With newfound independence came newfound responsibility. I had to consult my log book and decide on a dosage, with my parent's guidance and approval of course. Every meal I ate, every shot I took, every blood sugar check went into the record book, helping me track the dragon's movements and plan my strategy to defeat it. Sometimes, though, big meals would daunt me. I had never learned how to count carbs—with the antiquated NPH/Humalog[1] insulin regimen, it wasn't necessary. I based my dosage on past history and guesswork.

Coming from a large family, I'd often go out to restaurants for family dinners. On one particular August evening, we went to Olive Garden. My dad and I arrived and sat in the waiting area, more a corridor than a room. A crush of people swarmed into the restaurant, each struggling to get the hostess's attention. "I'll get to you in a moment!" she

---

[1] NPH insulin is an intermediate-acting insulin (meaning it peaks or activates a few hours after injection). Humalog is a fast-acting insulin (meaning it activates and begins to work as soon as it is injected).

called out. My father finally received a black square with flashing red lights around it after informing the hostess that we had a party of seventeen. "It'll be a little while," she said, sounding a bit flustered. We took our buzzer and went outside into the warm, humid summer air. Those buzzers always fascinated me, how the hostess could send a signal remotely and make the thing vibrate and flash.

Other family members arrived and when our table was ready, I sidled close to my cousin Rich. We had important things to discuss. "See any aliens lately?" I asked him under my breath. We were middle school and high school students by day, alien hunters by night. I wondered if maybe they had brought the dragon to earth. I had to find out.

"Not lately," he answered. "But I've seen some pretty strange things around my house."

I put my finger to my lips. "Not here, wait until we're inside."

He nodded.

An aromatic cloud of sauces, baked goods, bread sticks, and Italian food surrounded the train of hungry Cunders as we filed in. The dragon stirred inside me as my own stomach rumbled. I checked my cooler bag, making sure I brought my antidote. *"That's amore!"* chimed from the speakers. The hostess led us to our own table, practically in our own section. A few other tables crowded around ours, with couples or families already enjoying their meals. Grandma Ann went to the head of the table, and the rest of us filed into the remaining seats. I sat next to Rich, my thoughts already turning to the notebook I kept of my alien hunting adventures.

I opened my mouth to tell him of my recent findings when our waiter came and plopped a menu in front of each of us. I perused the options while the waiter mentioned a few specials. Bread sticks and soup, that's what I waited for. But what else? Pastas, soups, chicken, ravioli all enticed me. I'd need to take a big shot. Should I use the thirty-unit syringe or one of the bigger, fifty-unit needles?

The waiter finally asked if I was ready to order, pulling a pen and notebook from his green apron. I asked Rich what he was getting. "Tour of Italy," he said.

"I'll go with that," I told the waiter. Chicken parmigiana, lasagna, and fettuccine alfredo. How can you go wrong?

"Excellent choice, sir. It comes with a soup, which kind would you like?"

"*Pasta e fagioli.*" Not too much sugar or carbs in that one, other than the beans.

"Very good sir. I'll take your menu. Thank you."

Between Rich and myself, we needed another basket of

breadsticks within minutes. After I finished my bowl of soup too, the dragon really started to growl. "Ok," I said, "time to quiet you down." I took out a fresh syringe along with a vial of NPH and Humalog insulins. I rolled the NPH bottle, agitating the milky residue that rested at its bottom, watching as it spread into the clear liquid, turning it cloudy. I drew the proper amount from each vial and pulled up my shorts. I glanced around. What if the waiter comes back as I inject myself? What if those people at the other table see me? What if they think there's something wrong with me? If I'm a drug addict? A heroin user? I wiped the injection site with an alcohol swab, its pungent odor overpowering the smell of the food. I better do it quick before anyone sees.

I stabbed myself with the needle, pressing the plunger down. The dragon calmed. I don't think that anyone looked. At least if they did, they didn't stare. Just as I pulled the syringe from my thigh, our waiter returned. "More soup— oh, pardon me." He eyed the needle in my hands and went to the other side of the table. Fire flashed across my cheeks as I hurriedly capped the syringe, pulled my pant leg down, and thrust the beige case with my insulin back into the cooler bag. The waiter eventually returned and asked if I wanted more soup. I shook my head and said I was fine.

By the time the main course arrived, the fire had left my

face and I dug into the food. If someone thought I was a drug addict…oh well. I guess in a way, I am. I'm addicted to my medicine because without it, the dragon inside me would win. And whatever else I do, I can never let that happen. At all costs I must fight the beast. If I am branded for it, then so be it. I will not let it win, whatever it takes.

Sometimes I go to the bathroom to take my injections. Sometimes I still do it right at the dinner table when I'm out with friends or family. Really, it depends on how lazy I am, if I want to bother getting up to go to the bathroom. I'm a bit of a germ freak, so I always have to wash my hands before I eat anyway. So if I'm going to the bathroom to do that, then I'll hop in a stall and give myself a quick shot while I'm there.

Sometimes there isn't a bathroom around, though, like when I'm on the boardwalk. I've since perfected the art of giving myself an injection while standing up without a table or counter of any kind. As long as there's a garbage can nearby, I can hold the insulin pen and all the required components in my hand. I'll pop off the cap to the pen, put that in my pocket. Hold the pen in my right hand. Tear open the alcohol swab, wipe off the pen tip. Grab the needle, rip off the foil, twist it on. Click to the dosage, hold up my shirt, wipe the site, inject the insulin, pull out, twist off the needle, find the cap and slip the pen right back in my pocket. Thirty seconds, tops, right on the boardwalk with everyone walking by. I hope no one looks, but even if they do, there's nothing I can do about it. When my friend Ryan gives himself injections in public, he stares at people who look at him, makes his face go slack. If they think he's injecting some new pre-filled heroin pen, then at least it's something to laugh at.

A New Battle Plan

Dr. Starkman mentioned to me once that the most dramatic innovation he's seen throughout his years of endocrinology came with the advent of home blood glucose monitoring. Lindy, one of my father's early girlfriends, also fought the dragon—a precursor to what he'd have to face when I came along. Lindy's battle challenged her much more than it challenges me, however. My dad told me how she would have to guess the level of her blood sugar, estimating how much insulin she'd need. To test blood glucose back in the day, before the simplification of home glucose monitoring systems in the late 1980s and early 90s, a hospital blood test was required. The Keto-Diastix urinalysis test strips remained the only home testing procedure accessible to most diabetics until Roche released the Accu-Chek meter and Bayer introduced its Glucometer Elite in 1993.

Though it took many years to perfect the science of test strips and meters that offer results in less than thirty seconds with less blood, diabetes innovations would soon take off rapidly, changing in tandem with the technology boom, influenced and supported by the advancements in computers and micro-chips. Already, insulin pumps have improved dramatically; soon, Dr. Starkman and my current endocrinologist expect to see a "closed-loop system," a "smart" pump that communicates directly with a glucose monitoring chip to essentially create a replacement pancreas. (Already the advent and advancement of Continuous Glucose Monitoring systems has brought the technology one step closer.) Because even though pancreas transplants are performed for diabetics with a severe lack of control, there are risks involved, as well as a lifetime of anti-rejection drugs so the host body doesn't attack the foreign organ. "The pancreas is smart, though," Dr. Starkman says. "To duplicate it would take a level of technology that we just don't have yet. We're close, but such a system has yet to be perfected," he said back in 2014.

I'm still a few steps behind it. I haven't even taken the leap to a pump yet. When diabetes became a part of my life and of my parents' lives, the insulin options remained limited. Dr. Starkman prescribed an NPH/Humalog regimen for me, and I grew up with that system. Most of you reading this book—anyone who hasn't had diabetes for more than ten years—may have never even heard of such insulins or such an antiquated system that required me to take a shot at approximately the same time each morning, and eventually a second shot the same time each evening. It required me to eat my meals at the same time every day, along with a snack in between. Such a regimen, though cumbersome, continued to be the best available option for some time, through elementary school and even into the beginning of Junior High School.

When I was eleven, sitting in his office for my routine check-up, I listened to Dr. Starkman talk about something new. "You know, AJ, there's a system out there called basal/bolus insulin therapy. I really think it would work well for you."

I perked my ears, interested but hesitant. "What's that, exactly?"

"Well instead of taking two shots each day of long-acting and fast-acting, you'd take one shot of basal insulin—which establishes your baseline and combats the sugar produced naturally by your liver—at the same time each day, and then another shot each time you eat as your bolus dosage."

"I think I'll stick with just two shots."

"But this would give you more freedom. You could eat when you want and what you want. You'd have to start counting carbs, though, which you really should be doing anyway."

I still said no. And I left the office that day without even considering the possibilities of this new insulin regimen. I knew my fight with the dragon, I knew what worked and what didn't work. Yes, NPH and Humalog could be limiting at times, but at least I found comfort in a familiar system, a system I knew and grew up with. A system that allowed me to keep my A1C[1] consistently between seven and eight. It helped me fight the dragon to the best of my ability.

Or so I thought. I didn't realize my ignorance until much later.

With NPH and Humalog as my antidote, I believed that I had the dragon under control. I expected to continue living my life with syringes, needles, vials of insulin that had to stay refrigerated. Insulated bags and ice packs had become commonplace, burdensome and yet also comforting. The clink of the vials when I rolled them, the feel of the plunger in the syringe, the tap of my fingernail against the barrel of the needle as I flicked out any air bubbles. All of this soothed me. And so I persisted in my comfort zone, refusing to step

---

[1] A1C (also called hemoglobin A1C, HbA1C, or glycohemoglobin) values range from 4% to over 10% with a non-diabetic range of 4-5.7% and an ideal target range for diabetics (according to the American Diabetes Association) of below 7.0%. A1C results of 8.5% or higher indicate increased risk of developing complications such as cardiovascular and kidney disease.

outside it, even at the continued encouragement of my doctor.

Another visit with Dr. Starkman. "AJ, I really think you could improve your control." Out of all his juvenile diabetic patients, only three still used NPH and Humalog. I was one of them.

"But isn't it good enough now?" I asked, trying to evade his prodding.

"Wouldn't you like to eat whenever you wanted?"

I ran my fingers through my hair. I needed a haircut soon.

My dad sat in the chair next to me, his hand leaning on the polished red wood of the arm rest. "Maybe you should think about it," he suggested.

I shrugged. "Well what would I need to do if I decided to do this?"

The dragon growled inside me. I didn't know if it would like this new system or not.

"Well," Dr. Starkman said, reaching into one of the many drawers that comprised his desk, "you would need to keep track of your meals with this sheet." He handed me a blank chart with a smattering of blank spaces, row and column headings, and labels such as *Breakfast, Snack, Lunch, Dinner; Blood Glucose morning (in mg/dl); Blood Glucose Evening; Blood Glucose Night.* "And you'll also need to check your blood sugar every three hours."

That sounded a little burdensome. More so than my current two-shots-a-day, check-before-meals.

"Just for a week. Then we'll figure out your insulin-to-carb ratios and your corrections ratios."

"Carb ratios?" My voice wavered.

"Yes, to calculate the correct dosage for your meal bolus, you'll need to count carbs."

My armpits started sweating. I already had to do enough math in school.

"How do I know how many carbs are in foods?"

"There are a ton of easy books to use out there, with indexes, nutrition information. And that's just for whatever you eat, say in a restaurant, that doesn't come in a box with all of the nutrition information on the side."

I squeezed my knee, rubbing my hands along the top of my legs. "Well...I don't know. Maybe."

"We'll think about it," my dad encouraged. "My concerns," he turned to Dr. Starkman, "are whether these new insulins have any detrimental side effects, or health effects, or anything like that."

Dr. Starkman shook his head. "Lantus has been approved for use since 2000. And if you like using syringes, you can still get both Lantus and NovoLog[1] in vials. Or, if you prefer convenience…" he pulled another goodie out of his desk. "There's a pen delivery system." He held up a dark blue cylinder a little thicker than his thumb. It had a cap on it with a clip and everything. Just like a pen.

He uncapped it and exposed a threaded tip. "You just screw on a needle cap here each time you use it, twist this dial at the end to the appropriate dosage, and inject it just like you would a syringe."

Interesting.

"And it doesn't have to be refrigerated after you open it," he added.

Now I'm listening.

"You just have to use it within thirty days, just like you would a regular vial.

This might just work.

"Ok," my dad said. "How about we keep this log of meals and numbers, and schedule a follow up?"

"We can do that." Dr. Starkman capped the pen, clicked the dial on the opposite end back to zero, and dropped it back into his drawer.

On the ride home, I thought. I thought. And I thought

---

[1] Lantus is a basal insulin, which means it acts steadily over a 24-hour period. NovoLog is a bolus insulin, which means it is fast-acting and begins working upon injection to lower blood sugar quickly

some more. What did this new system mean for me? *Change.*
I hated change. *But it could be a good change. A better
change.* More shots? How could more shots be *good?* But
would those additional injections help me to better fight the
dragon? Maybe.

And what about school? With this new system, I'd have
to take shots at school before lunch. How would that work?
Well, you keep insulin in the fridge, or in your box, and
inject yourself at the nurse's office when you check your
blood sugar. You already go there every day before lunch
anyway.

But what if other students see me taking a shot? What
will they think?

Just go to the bathroom and take it there.

If I injected in my butt or leg I *would* have to go to the
bathroom. But wait. Legs and butt and arm. Three injection
sites. My battle strategies—my injection site rotation
plans—wouldn't allow me to inject in the same site more
than twice a day. I counted on my fingers. *Morning, lunch,
snack, dinner, Lantus...* That's more than three injections for
only three sites.

What about your stomach?

My eyes widened and I shook my head. Never. Inject in
my stomach? No, I can't do that. What if I hit an organ? Or

go too close to my belly button? Or what if I stab one of my solid abs?

As if they really are solid. Don't worry, there's plenty of subcutaneous fat there.

Maybe a centimeter. But what if the needle pierces a rib?

Don't inject so high.

An answer for everything.

*****

A few days later, I wanted to go to Ray's Sport Shop, a store that catered to outdoor enthusiasts as well as law enforcement professionals. That stuff always interested me. It was always my dream to be a police officer (and a Special Agent—I think I mentioned that already), and because of the dragon I was nearly denied the chance to become one. (I explained some of it—the rest I'll tell you about in a later chapter).

In preparation for my anticipated career, I started collecting all kinds of police gear and equipment. Just to play around with, and dress up with, pretending I was a cop. I'd "pull my dad over" in the living room, using my voice as a siren, holding a yellow notepad and pretending it was a ticket book. He saved some of those early citations. I think I gave him one once for talking too loudly on the piano bench he was "driving."

And just to be fair to another dream profession of mine, I had my own set of kid-sized fire fighter turnout gear too. I had to be impartial, after all, and dress up as a cop one day and as a fire fighter the next. At the time, I wasn't sure which one I wanted to be. I was also considering as possible professions: paleontology (who doesn't like dinosaurs?), financial advising (because that's what my dad did), and meteorology (which I thought was a nice gig, to just study the weather without any penalty for being wrong). I even told my dad that I'd be a police officer on Monday, a meteorologist on Tuesday, a financial advisor on Wednesday, a paleontologist on Thursday, and take the day off on Friday. I liked my long weekends.

So, I packed up my diabetes bag after eating breakfast, in case the dragon should grow restless, and made sure to record what I ate, the carb amount, my morning insulin dosage, and my blood glucose on the special log sheet. Then my dad and I hopped into the car and drove to North Plainfield.

The flashing red police light in the front window of the store caught my attention, and I watched the revolving, flashing beam for a minute or so, wondering how it would look on the dashboard of my car one day. When I got a car.

I couldn't even drive yet. After that exhausted my interest, I stepped inside, and the musty smell of old hunting jackets hit me in the face. The aged wood of the entrance gave the store a cabin-in-the-forest kind of feel. Works of taxidermy lined the walls of the showroom, stuffed wolves peering down from their perches, deer staring blankly with glassy black eyes, turkeys frozen in the midst of ruffling their feathers, a bear standing on his hind legs atop a stump, a silent growl parting his lips and baring his teeth. I searched for a dragon, but couldn't find one.

I browsed through the gun section of the store, weaving my way through the glass vaults of thousand-dollar hunting rifles and shotguns, scanning the counters of handguns: revolvers, automatics, blue, gray, silver, 9mm, .45, Smith and Wesson, Ruger, Glock, Sig Sauer, Colt. I glanced at some price tags. $1,000 for a piece of metal and plastic. I left the gun room and went to the police equipment section. I needed a new duty belt for my outfit. I ran my hands through the hanging leather straps, and finally found one that looked decent. A Velcro closure fastened it rather than a buckle, and it felt thick and sturdy enough to support all my gear. I tried it on, strapping it around my waist. I needed a smaller size. That's generally the problem with a fourteen-year-old kid shopping in an adult store. Eventually I dug up the smallest size they had and discovered that, with enough clothes on and another belt underneath, it fit pretty well. I tried to convince my dad that I needed it.

"How much is it?"

"Fifty."

"You don't need that! What do you need that for?"

"The one I have is too small."

He examined it, checked the stitching, tried the Velcro. "You really want it?"

I bobbed my head up and down.

"Maybe it can be an early Christmas present. Or maybe you'll just have to wait until Christmas to play with it."

I stuck out my lower lip, but couldn't say more. At least he'd buy it for me.

Back in the car, on our way home. I glanced at the clock.

"Time to check," Dad said. I rummaged through my bag, searching for my meter. My meter…

Damn. I forgot my meter at home.

"Um, I think I forgot it."

"What?" he said. "You're kidding."

"On the counter."

He nearly stopped the car, his eyes flaring. "You're kidding." As if repeating it could make it true. I knew that wasn't good. I knew his anger began to boil. Like it did in the doctor's office all those years ago. "Dammit, AJ. You can't be stupid. You have to check yourself every three hours for this. Now it's going to be off."

The anger that he once directed toward my pediatrician was about to be directed at me. But I was used to it. It wasn't anything new. Only fair that what once saved my life would come back to haunt me. Nothing comes without a price.

"I'm sorry." It's the only thing I could think of.

"Sorry doesn't cut it. Sorry doesn't check your blood sugar. You can't be an idiot."

"It'll only be an hour off."

"Doesn't matter, dammit! Dr. Starkman said every three hours. This is your life. How can you be so G-D stupid that you forgot your meter? You know you have to check every three hours!"

I clenched my fists. I wanted to punch him. It felt like he wanted to punch me. I tried to disappear in the leather seats of the car.

Wrestling the dragon seemed like a breeze compared to battling my father. I checked myself when I got home. I put it in the log book with a note that it wasn't exactly three hours after breakfast. Dr. Starkman later said it was fine, nothing to worry about.

*****

After resisting the change for so long, I finally gave in to Dr. Starkman's recommendation and switched to the basal/bolus system. It was the best choice I made in terms of diabetes self-management. I sat through the consultation with the dietician, practiced using the insulin pens, got the new prescriptions for Lantus and NovoLog, looked through the nutritional book and marked the pages that had food I ate a lot. Fifteen carbs for a slice of bread, thirty carbs for a medium apple. Ninety carbs for a big plate of pasta. One unit of NovoLog insulin for every ten carbs, one unit for every thirty blood glucose points over my target of 100 mg/dl. Thirty-four units of Lantus every day at dinner-time.

When the new pens came, I looked at them, intrigued. A few days later, on the night before I was scheduled to officially switch over, my blood sugar was a little high. I opened one of the fresh packs, screwed on a needle, twisted the dial. And decided to face my fears head on. I'd have to start using my stomach as an injection site, so why not use it for my very first shot with the new pen. I wiped the site with alcohol, pinched it—somewhat disconcerted that I had so much extra fat there—and the short needle slipped in.

It actually didn't feel so bad. I barely felt it at all. I pushed the plunger down, each click marking off one unit.

Waited for a while to make sure there wouldn't be any leakage, probably longer than I had to. Took it out. Massaged my stomach. And never again had a fear of injecting insulin there.

At school, I'd take my shot in the stomach. I even brought a pre-made list of how much insulin I'd have to take at lunch, depending on what they were serving that day. I still have that list, tucked away in a cupboard with other diabetes relics. Like the beige case I used to keep my insulin vials and syringes in.

A few months after starting the regimen—and with a few adjustments and tweaks along the way—my A1C was down to seven. By the next year, it was down to six and change. I've even had a few that were 5.9 and 5.8. This system was definitely a better way to fight the dragon, and I admit I should've accepted it sooner. The dragon lost nearly all his control over me as I could finally enjoy the dietary freedom of other kids. I could finally go up on the boardwalk with my cousins and eat an ice cream cone, not because it was part of my snack or my dinner insulin dosage, but simply because it was what I wanted—no time restrictions, no carb restrictions, no sugar limitations. I finally enjoyed a life I had previously never even dared to dream of, and I berated myself for letting the fear of change almost prevent me from taking this glorious plunge—that almost stopped me from discovering what it was like to eat what I wanted, when I wanted it. Just like every other non-diabetic kid.

A Low Blow from the

Dragon

Spectators and combatants filled the high school gymnasium for Grand Master Ye Bong Choi's annual Tae Kwon Do tournament. I carried my huge bag filled with sparring gear—it was nearly as big as I was, stuffed with a *hogu* (protective chest pad), foam forearm guards, shin guards, foam helmet, instep guards. I wondered if I could use them when I fought the dragon but figured they wouldn't really be much use. For that I carried my own customary accessories—Juicy Juice boxes, beige insulin case in a cooler bag with an ice pack, water bottle, and some snacks. When I was all geared up, I looked like a marshmallow. Or the Michelin Man. We all did—those of us who were there to compete in the sparring competitions, anyway. My cousin Rich, my cousin Molly, and myself. My dad's own posse. (He's a Master—fifth degree black belt—and he used to train the three of us in our basement).

We wove through the sections, finding an open spot on the bleachers to stow our gear as the smells of cheap hot dogs, hamburgers, and concession snacks mingled with sweaty feet and dirty socks. I stretched my hamstrings in my loose-fitting Tae Kwon Do *gi*, cracking my neck and mentally preparing myself for the moment I'd face my opponent. "What do I get if I win first place?" I asked my dad.

He gave me a look and said, "What do you want this time?"

Let's see, last tournament I won I got a video game. "I think there's a new iPod coming out. How about that?"

"Okay," he agreed after some finagling.

"What about if I get second place?"

"Come on, now, Age. Only if you get first-place. That's the deal."

"Fine," I grumbled, straightening the red belt around my waist and going over the different kicks and punches in my mind. Front kick, back kick, side kick, round-house. Reverse punch, jab. I watched other sparring matches, surreptitiously surveilled the other kids registered in the 12-14 age group.

This tournament worked with point systems for the free sparring matches. One point for a kick or punch to the chest area. Two points for a successful kick to the head (without hitting too hard, or a penalty could be issued). The first competitor to reach three points wins.

The announcer's voice boomed over the loudspeakers, summoning the youth sparring competitors to the competition area of the gymnasium, past the area where martial artists performed amazing feats of flying kicks and Tae Kwon Do forms that looked like elaborate dances, hands and feet moving like lightning.

"Good luck, guys," my dad said, getting ready to cheer us on. My cousin Rich went to his ring, Molly went to hers, and I put in my mouth guard, sucking on the sour rubber. "Remember, Age, hit hard and hit fast." My dad demonstrated a reverse punch (as if I could've forgotten how to execute the proper move). "Don't let him intimidate you."

Easier said than done. I swallowed my nerves and adjusted the Velcro straps on my forearm and shin guards, slipping my fingers through the hand protectors that weren't quite boxing mitts. I sipped down a whole Juicy Juice box to make sure my blood sugar wouldn't go low—but then I started thinking, what if it does? What if I start to feel dizzy right in the middle of the sparring match? What if I pass out in front of all these people? What if the dragon distracts me, and I miss a kick or a punch, or I can't block an attack because I'm too busy dodging the dragon's fire?

No. That's what the juice was for. But then what if my blood sugar goes high because of my nerves and adrenaline? What's the right balance? What—

"Anthony Cunder!" the referee summoned me to the center of the ring. "Kwon Davis!"

We bowed to each other. I looked him in the eyes for a second before averting my gaze. He looked fierce. Angry. But not nearly as ferocious as the dragon.

"*Sijak!*" the referee commanded. *Begin.*

My opponent threw punches like a wild beast, and it was all I could do to back away, defending. I couldn't find an opening, and pushed him back with a side kick. Did he land any punches? I couldn't tell, my heart was pounding so hard. The referee didn't yell "*Kalyeo*", which would order us to stop, so I kept going, circling, keeping my distance as I evaluated my opponent. Was he reckless? Quick to throw punches that would leave his chest exposed? Could I try a kick to his head? He was about my height. I was flexible enough, I thought.

I zoned out the rest of the gymnasium, focused on one thing, one object—my opponent. My dad always told me he would yell things at me, tell me what to do from the sideline. But I never heard him. I never heard anything but the blood rushing in my ears, the sound of my fist or foot striking a protective pad. The yell—the *kihap*—that exploded from my gut.

And the flurry of punches returned, Kwon pushing me back into a corner.

"*Kalyeo!*" the ref yelled. "One point, blue!" He gestured to my opponent whose *hogu* showed blue circles. Mine showed red.

"Come on!" My dad tried to argue on my behalf. "Those weren't even real punches!"

But the ref wouldn't listen. The two corner refs saw the point too. He held out his hand, and I faced Kwon once more. "*Sijak!*"

This time I went on the offensive, throwing my own burst of punches and kicks and everything else I had in me, pushing him back, something would land, past his own attacks, he never even blocked, he never even—

"*Kalyeo!*" the command came again. "One point!" This time he pointed to me, and I smiled. I wondered how Kwon liked it when he got a taste of his own technique.

"Come on, work it Kwon!" someone yelled from the sidelines.

One-to-one. Time to roll.

"*Sijak!*"

We circled each other, waiting, watching, our hands up

to protect ourselves, to guard, to take advantage of the opening the other would create with a reckless attack.

We couldn't wait too long, though, or the referee could assign a penalty for stalling.

So I went for it. One kick to the head, and I'd win. I made my approach, knees soft, left foot in front, edging closer, struck—and felt his punch land in my gut, knocking the wind out of me. I stumbled back. Did my foot make contact? I wasn't sure. I hit something, I knew that. But was it his shoulder, his neck, his arm? Those wouldn't count. Only the head.

"*Kalyeo!*" The moment of truth. "One point!" He gestured to Kwon. If I didn't get a point too, then I'd have to catch up. He'd be one point away from winning.

The ref pulled his hands together, summoning us to the center.

I must not have made contact.

"Wait," one of the corner referees said. Two more pairs of eyes watched the match, in case the lead ref missed something. "I saw red connect his kick." He looked to the third ref. "Master Chin?"

"Yes," he nodded. "Red connected. Two points."

"If two referees saw the point, then two points red," the lead ref said, and a surge of adrenaline washed through me.

"Winner, red!" he said, holding up my hand.

"Yeah, Age!" my dad yelled. I tossed him my foam helmet. "How do you feel? Do you feel low? Want some juice?"

I shook my head, but then reconsidered. That was a tough match. The dragon started to uncoil in my belly, shake its wings. "Yeah, maybe another box."

He popped in the straw, and I sipped it down.

I had some time before I'd have to spar again. My dad and I watched my cousins fight. They won their matches too, and then back in the ring I went. Back to focusing, shutting out the world as I watched my opponent, attacked, defended, sucked air into my lungs to satiate their cry as I battled. This guy wouldn't hold me back from that trophy. From that new iPod. The dragon wouldn't hold me back.

Time always seemed to simultaneously fly and slow down when I sparred, when my concentration intensified so I felt every fiber in my body, every sinew and muscle tightened, my senses heightened. I blinked away sweat dripping down my forehead.

I got a punch in. He got a kick. I got another punch. He got a kick. Tie match.

We went at it, evenly matched. He kept his guard up, knew how to block. His strikes were precise, targeted, calculated. Maybe he wanted something, too. Maybe his dad promised him a new iPod, or computer, or video game.

Punch, kick, back kick, side kick combo. Front leg, back leg, push him back, reevaluate, reengage. I couldn't let him get another point. It had to be my point.

A flurry of attacks, his, mine, all scrambled together.

"*Kalyeo!*"

The moment of hesitation, calculation. Would the ref award a point, or was he just breaking us up to re-center, to start again? He pointed to the starting positions. "Ready? *Sijak!*" And it began again, until I saw the perfect opening. He went for a front leg side kick, and I executed my favorite move: the back kick. A 180 degree spin on the ball of the front foot, point the heel of the rear foot and snap it forward.

It connected. I felt it. My opponent felt it. The referees felt it as my competitor flew back, nearly out of bounds.

"*Kalyeo!* One point, red! Winner, red!"

My hand went up, and I climbed the tournament ladder— one step closer to my prize.

"Nice one, AJ," my cheerleader said as he asked if I wanted more juice.

"Yeah, and a graham cracker. Two crackers." That was always one of my staple snacks. Honey Maid Cinnamon (or honey, but I much preferred cinnamon).

The dragon rumbled, tasting the stale, sweet cinnamon through my tongue. Maybe it was too much. Didn't really feel low. But I was hungry, and I had an excuse to eat.

I shouldn't have done it, though.

Molly came over—she won all of her matches—and Rich would be going home with a second-place trophy.

I had one more match. I was guaranteed at least second place.

"Are you sure I can't get the iPod if I come in second?" I asked my dad one final time as I put in my mouth guard, swallowing those final, sweet crumbs. The molding was always a little bit off—I don't think I bit down on it properly when I first got it, so it forever misaligned my teeth when I used it. "Maybe a smaller iPod?"

He shook his head. "First place was the deal. I have faith in you. Look at that guy, you can beat him. You watched him fight. He likes to go for the fancy moves, so just wait until you see an opening and take it. A good, solid reverse punch right to the chest. Pow!" He snapped his fist.

Armored for battle, I sauntered into the ring, eyeing the referees, my opponent, the stands full of spectators who would disappear in moments when the ref signaled us to begin. I adjusted my straps one final time, thoughts of a shiny new iPod glimmering in my mind.

And then the ineffable tingle of high blood sugar worked its way through my veins. My mouth went dry, and a fuzziness shrouded my thoughts—never quite as acute as hypoglycemia, but noticeable nevertheless.

"Ready?" the ref asked my opponent.

"Ready?" the ref asked me.

I wondered how long it would take for me to check my blood sugar, take a shot of insulin. Too long. And everyone would see me, wonder why I left the ring just as the match was about to start. Would they think I was afraid, trying to run away?

I hesitated a moment before nodding.

The ref's hand between us, my opponent's eyes focused and intent, a slight pain scratching at my stomach, the dragon growling and clawing.

"*Sijak!*"

The blows came fast and furious, and I backed to the edge of the ring.

If you need time or space, just step out of bounds, my dad's voice echoed in my mind. Don't run out, otherwise you can get a penalty. Make it look like an accident.

I didn't do it, though. I stayed inside the tape as I fended off my attacker, wondering how, when I could launch a counterattack. He kicked, and I blocked it; he punched, I sidestepped it; his foot whistled through the air in a spinning back hook kick and it slammed into the side of my head.

"*Kalyeo!*" I didn't even have to guess who got that point. Or two points. "Two points, blue!"

Already behind, and this was only the first contact. The dragon tried to distract me, weigh me down, turn my fists and feet into lead.

I just had to focus. Forget about the dragon. Soon. Soon it would be over and I could check my sugar, satiate my body's cry for insulin. Maybe if I exercised hard enough, my sugar would go down on its own.

Or I could throw the match. Let him win so it could be over and I could take my antidote, dilute the dragon's poison in my blood that weakened me.

But then I wouldn't get my iPod. And weakness turned to anger. Why did the dragon have to do this to me? Why, why couldn't I be like everyone else?

The instant the ref yelled, "*Sijak!*" I flew into a frenzy, kicking and punching my opponent as if he were the dragon itself.

"*Kalyeo!*" came the command moments later.

I didn't get a point. My opponent had just gone out of bounds. He used my dad's trick. Or maybe I pushed him out of bounds.

Again, I channeled my anger at the dragon towards the enemy I could strike, but I controlled myself this time. I landed a punch. And another. And another. I felt them connect with the *hogu*, heard the dull *thud* of foam on foam.

I got a point this time. Too bad they couldn't accumulate.

Two points blue, one point red.

"*Sijak!*"

A kick this time, right from the starting block. But he kicked too, and our legs connected mid-air. Again, we both kicked and smashed our shins. The next time I waited, and when he executed a side kick I slipped under his guard with a *pichigi* kick, coming forward with my back foot and slicing up at a forty-five degree angle.

A solid connection. It felt like his kick might have landed, but it would be up to the refs to decide if we both got a point.

I said a quick prayer while the referees deliberated.

Then the lead red said, "One point, red!"

I melted with relief, and the dragon growled.

Soon. Just one more point. Either way, just one more point.

Then came the final round.

"*Sijak!*"

We circled, waiting, watching. I couldn't wait too long,

though, or my anger would fade—the anger giving me energy.

Front leg *pichigi*, back kick, side kick combo.

Did anything connect? The refs didn't see it. We kept going.

He threw a punch, I threw another kick; he kicked, I punched.

"*Kalyeo!*"

Whose point was it? Who would win first place?

"One point, red!"

And the iPod was mine.

The dragon didn't win.

I ran to my dad and said I should check my blood sugar. It was 300.

The rush of insulin I took in the bathroom calmed me, satiated me, satisfied the dragon inside me for the moment.

Should I have stopped and checked my glucose as soon as I felt my blood sugar rising? Probably. Even though high blood sugar isn't as immediately threatening as low blood sugar, it still isn't healthy. It can fatigue you in its own way, make it feel like you have fire in your blood or cotton in your throat. Not to mention the organ damage from prolonged hyperglycemia.

Would I have felt embarrassed to be singled out, or have

the match postponed because of me? Absolutely. But when I stood up with the other medalists and trophy winners—as they called out my name for winning first place in the 12 – 14-year-old red belt category—I smiled, just like I smiled a few years later after earning my black belt, and I imagined what my new iPod would look like, knowing that, even though the dragon tried to distract me, I was able to overcome it.

Diet Soda? Not This Time

I had never flown before. Well, I had flown to Florida when I was an infant, shortly after the dragon came to live inside me. But I don't remember anything of that trip, nor anything of the plane ride. So to me, this plane ride felt like my first.

The Morris County Sheriff's Explorer Post #140 prepared to embark on a trip to Fort Collins, Colorado to participate in the 2008 National Law Enforcement Exploring Conference, an event held every two years that consisted of competitions, conventions, expos, and a jolly good time. As explorers, we got an inside look into the world of law enforcement. Sponsored by the Boy Scouts of America, Explorer Posts welcome youths aged fourteen – twenty-one who are interested in learning about the work of law enforcement officers. Posts are organized and run by individual law enforcement agencies, ranging from local police departments and county sheriff's offices to federal agencies like U.S. Customs and Border Protection and the FBI.

As an explorer, I met with the twenty other members of

my post at the Morris County Public Safety Training Academy each Monday where we had our own Physical Training sessions, classroom instruction on various aspects of law enforcement, and hands-on training in police work such as motor vehicle stops, responding to calls of home break-ins, robberies, first aid, and domestic violence to name a few. Sixteen of us would attend this National Conference and compete in various categories. Each post designated teams of four to participate in the competitions, with first, second, and third place trophies awarded to the posts who performed to the highest standards in each scenario.

But our trip wouldn't consist entirely of the National Conference. We planned a bit of a vacation for the week leading up to the conference, and so we arrived at the Newark Liberty International Airport with the competitions in the backs of our minds—for the moment.

The morning sun was a fiery red ball by the time we wheeled our luggage through the airport entrance. In addition to my duffel bag, I also carried a bright red bag that contained all the diabetes supplies I'd need for the trip along with a letter from Dr. Starkman. I kept another copy folded in my pocket, a letter of passage that would permit me to pass the inspectors at the toll (or *troll*) bridge. Without it, I'd never be able to bring the Juicy Juice or my medicine onto the plane. My bracelet also encircled my left wrist, a med-alert band that chained me to the dragon and the dragon to me.

I nudged Ryan's arm, a bracelet around his wrist as well. He fought the dragon too, a legacy passed down from his ancestors. His family crest, a shield topped by the head of a knight and the hilts of two swords, tattooed across his back while a dragon perched on his left shoulder, the beast surrounded by the words *Truth, Honor, Justice.*

"Got your letter?" I asked.

"Yup. Right here."

"Busy airport for six in the morning, isn't it?" I asked.

He rolled his shoulders. "I guess so."

"Oh. This is my first time in an airport. First time flying."

"It's not so bad," he said.

Ryan planned to run this year for National Youth Explorer Representative, the chairman and liaison between the national explorer board and all the explorer posts across the country. Each explorer post at the National Conference would cast its vote for one of three candidates, and the winner would serve a term of two years. We brought posters with us, helped Ryan with his campaign speech, made flyers, and prayed that he'd win. I was sure that he would. Even with the dragon. He wouldn't let the dragon hold him back.

We checked our baggage, got our tickets, and made our way to the appropriate gate. The TSA checkpoint loomed. I checked my papers of passage once more. The line twisted and turned through the barricades.

My turn came, and I took off my belt and shoes, put them in a plastic bin along with my backpack, and readied my letter. The agents' stark white uniforms shone in the fluorescent lighting. "Ok, step through," one said. I didn't look at him, kept my eyes down, the paper crinkling in my hand.

Some commotion behind the x-ray station. They call another TSA agent over.

"Sir," another said to me, "please step over here." A trickle of sweat ran down my back. Not from the dragon this time.

"Yes?"

"You know you can't bring liquid over three-point-four ounces."

"Yes, I'm diabetic though, I need those juice boxes in case my blood sugar goes low." I handed him the letter. He squinted at it, showed it to a different agent, called over a supervisor.

They looked through everything else in my bag, searching every compartment.

A few minutes later, they nodded, handing me back my letter. "Ok, no problem."

Ryan snuck in behind me, handed them his letter, and they waved him through.

We rushed to catch up to the rest of our group. Advisor Campbell—our post leader, an officer with the sheriff's department—didn't wait for us as the rest of the group filtered past and continued to the gate.

We did catch up, and I was amazed by the conveyor belts for people. The shops along the corridor buzzed with activity, waking me up despite my frequent yawns. At least I'd get to sleep on the plane.

Or at the gate, as it turned out. We had another hour before our plane accepted boarders, and I nearly dozed off despite the flutter of excitement within me. Conversations flitted between my fellow explorers, but I stayed quiet. "AJ! Why do you talk so much?" Lucas joked. I just laughed and shrugged, fidgeting. It wasn't the first time—or last—that someone made a comment about my reserved nature.

The stewardess finally announced, "We'll be boarding in fifteen minutes. Elderly and disabled, please move to the front for priority boarding, followed by rows fifty through thirty-five. Thank you."

Did I qualify as disabled? No, probably not in this sense.

Our turn came, and I entered the ambiguous, intestine-like tunnel. I stepped over the threshold and wrinkled my nose at the smell of cheap plastic and soiled carpet. I pushed down the aisle to my window seat and tucked my med bag underneath, my backpack sandwiched between my legs. Didn't want my computer getting lost or stolen. The engines of the plane rumbled, and I looked out at the gray pavement of the runway. Eventually, we started moving, the rumble growing louder. My seat overlooked the back of the plane's wing, and the flaps fluttered. The plane's speed increased, inertia pushed me back into my seat. I checked my seatbelt, tightening the straps. What was it the flight attendant had said during the introductory speech? Something about our seatbelts. I should have paid attention.

My hand clutched the armrest as a shudder rifled through the plane. The wings jerked, and the front wheel left the ground, slanting us upward, angling towards the skies, towards the heavens. Gravity tried to pull us down, keep us on the earth, but the plane's engines roared. The ground blurred, shrinking and blending into an indistinct pattern, a three-dimensional map, a dragon's-eye view that transformed what once looked so familiar into a nearly unrecognizable world full of slow-moving dots and busy ant hills. The Captain's voice came over the speakers, belting out some statistics: plane's velocity, wind speed and direction, and how long he expected it to take to get to Colorado. I started to pull the seatbelt release, but then decided against it.

Shannon and Rick, the explorers next to me, threw off their belts and twisted in their seats, struggling to find a comfortable niche. I stared out the window, tapping the thick pane. Clouds floated beneath us, before us, behind us, and around us, some curly white wisps, others thick cumulus cotton balls. As we headed west, the forests and labyrinths of streets and cities gave way to open plains, vast square fields divided at right angles by roads and highways. I squirmed in my seat. I had to pee, but I didn't want to get up and bother the two next to me. The dilemma of having a window seat, I lamented silently.

Two or three hours later, the pilot's voice crackled over the speakers again. "Good afternoon everyone. It is now one pm Mountain Time, and we'll be landing in Denver shortly. Please remember to follow all instructions given by the flight attendants and crew, and remember to fasten your seatbelts when the seatbelt light illuminates. Also please remember to remove all baggage from the aisles and from under the seats beneath or in front of you, stowing everything in the luggage compartments overhead. Thank you for flying with us, and we hope to see you again."

I checked my seatbelt, tugging on the straps until it pressed tightly against my waist. My backpack sagged tiredly on the floor. It didn't want to get up, and I didn't either, so I just tucked it between my feet and hugged it with my knees.

In the Denver airport, we navigated the terminals to the baggage claim, and I waited for my orange and black rolling suitcase. The other explorers picked up their luggage. And still I waited. Three revolutions. Four. Haven't I seen this brown suitcase pass ten times already? The number of bags on the metal merry-go-round dwindled. Two of us still didn't have our baggage. I looked around for the lost suitcase claims room. "How long will this take?" I said with a nervous crack in my voice when finally the familiar orange material caught my eye. I smiled as the ice melted from my chest and my heart returned to its normal cadence.

As soon as I stepped outside, the crisp, clean air of the mountains hit me, filling my lungs with a fresh, pristine burst that purified the contaminants and smog of the city air I'd breathed my entire life. I stuffed my bags into the rental van and piled in along with a handful of other explorers. We barely fit, and I imagined this was what a clown car felt like. Country music blared on the radio.

After an hour-long drive, we pulled into the parking lot of our motel. The outside looked nice, but we couldn't see any pool. Campbell went to the front desk while we waited in the van, the summer heat crisping us despite the open windows. Tony hooked up his iPod using an FM transmitter. His playlist ran through ten songs as we waited.

"What is taking them so long?" Lucas cried, wiping the sweat from his forehead.

"I don't know," Ryan said. "Must be some problem."

"Well why don't they just flash their badges?" I suggested. "Doesn't that always work?"

Campbell finally returned. "This place is disgusting," he said with a sneer. "Nothing like the pictures online." We filtered out of the vans and peeked into one of the open rooms. One of the girls with us screamed.

"So are we staying here?" Ryan asked, wrinkling his nose at some rancid odor.

Campbell spat, lighting up a cigarette. "Na, we'll go somewhere else." He puffed a cloud of smoke into the air.

"But what about our deposits?" Tony asked.

"I'll get them back." More smoke.

Into the vans we piled once again, and traversed Nevada Ave until we passed another motel, a Rodeway Inn & Suites. "This one looks promising," Ryan offered as we pulled under an archway with the blue, rectangular Rodeway sigil at its center. This one had a pool, a nice pool with crystalline blue waters sparkling beside the parking lot.

I jumped out and ran to look at one of the open rooms, a maid arranging the bed sheets.

"At least this one doesn't smell bad," Ryan murmured next to me. Campbell talked to the proprietor and discovered that the inn had enough vacancies for all of us. And a continental breakfast was included.

Campbell started assigning rooms. "Taylor, Cunder, room one-oh-one with me. Gotta keep the diabetic kids together." He looked in the van. "Lucas too, you're with us."

I grabbed my bags and zipped off to the room, settling them beside the bed and securing a spot in the fridge for my insulin. I made sure Ryan had room for his too. Campbell took the bed closest to the window with Ryan, leaving the other one for Lucas and me.

That night I hugged the edge of the mattress. I was afraid of rolling off, but I was also afraid of rolling the other way too. This was the first time I had slept in a bed with anyone who wasn't related to me. So I woke myself up with every twitch and turn, barely getting any sleep. Apparently, I remained within my boundaries, though, because Campbell commented on it the next morning. "You didn't move much last night," he said during his morning cigarette. "Stayed straight as a board."

"Oh." I shrugged. "Good to know."

That day our vacation really began. We had some activities scheduled, including a visit to the Garden of the Gods. As we prepared to leave, I checked my black ditty bag for my insulin and for my juice boxes—I know, a high school kid with Juicy Juice. But I didn't know anything else, and that's what my parents had given me my entire life.

All in order, except… *Damn.* One of the juice boxes had sprung a leak, spewing its sweet, sticky liquid all over everything in my bag. I took out the juice box along with whatever else it soiled—spare t-shirt, napkins, map of the city. *Damn.* Now what? I always took juice boxes with me, that's what the dragon loved best when it started to growl. I couldn't just feed it fruit bars, that would take too long when I needed quick sugar.

Erika, one of our other post advisors, called out, "Everyone ready? White van's heading out in five."

Would glucose tablets be enough? No, not if we did any strenuous physical activity—walking, running, hiking, climbing—a simple sleeve of glucose tablets would never last. Another juice box? That could just leak again. I needed something else.

"Anyone want green tea?" Campbell shouted. "We got five cases of it!"

"I'll take diet," I said, tucking a bottle in my bag.

"Not regular?" Campbell asked.

"I never drink regular. My blood sugar would go high."

I had a foot over the threshold when I stopped. In a moment, it dawned on me. My epiphany. A solution that would solve the dilemma of sticky, leaking juice boxes that never fit in my pocket, of not having enough tablets on me to combat low blood sugar. *Regular* Lipton Green Tea! Why had I never thought of it before?

"Actually, I'll take one," I said, turning back. "Or two."

"Here, we got plenty."

I stuffed a few bottles into my bag, and from that day forward, my strategy to combat the dragon's hypoglycemic growl changed forever.

Everyone hopped into the vans, and off we went to the Garden of the Gods that wasn't really a garden, but rather a vast formation of rock. The clear blue sky did nothing to block out the sun, and the hat on my head did even less to dampen the heat. Yet, the dark red rocks that jutted from the ground in fantastic, convoluted shapes made the excursion worthwhile. One formation resembled two camels kissing, the tips of their noses pressed together, two heads emerging from the solid rock around them.

A gray steel plaque on another rock read,

THE GARDEN OF THE GODS

GIVEN TO
THE CITY OF COLORADO SPRINGS
IN 1909
BY THE CHILDREN
OF
CHARLES ELLIOTT PERKINS

IN FULFILLMENT OF HIS WISH
THAT IT BE KEPT FOREVER
FREE TO THE PUBLIC

Some of us climbed the rock formations, gathering upon their summits like insects exploring the terrain. Others preferred to hide under ledges, escaping the heat, sprawled on the cool stone. I joined the adventurers, exerting my energy, working my muscles, stretching my arms and digging my toes into whatever crevices I could find. After half an hour, I knew the dragon would soon stir. I cracked open the seal of my green tea bottle, the *pop* of the plastic tabs awakening the dragon from its slumber. I twisted off the dark green cap and took my first (intentional)[1] sip of a

---

[1] A few times before, I'd gone to restaurants with my mother and ordered a diet soda (my father seldom let me drink soda, even diet) and the waiter or waitress accidentally brought regular. I could usually tell, after the first sip, and my parents usually carried Keto-Diastix to double

regular soft drink.

My tongue marveled at the sugary taste, and a rush of exhilaration shot through me. *I'm actually drinking a regular drink! A regular drink, just like everyone else.* Nothing against diet, but artificial sweeteners never really thrilled me. Thinking back on it now, though, the high fructose corn syrup was probably just as bad. I didn't know about that then, though.

I took a few more sips, then capped the bottle and slipped it back into my bag. I couldn't drink all of it, I had to save some in case the dragon growled later. And I had to walk a careful line, balancing exercise and sugar so the dragon wouldn't get angry. I couldn't have too much, or my blood sugar would go high. When we got back to the Rodeway Motel, my reading was 105 mg/dl. We went on to the conference at Colorado State University (after some more sightseeing and white-water rafting—I made sure to stock plenty of green tea bottles in the raft and hoped they didn't fall out when we went over the choppy rapids); Ryan won the election for National Youth Representative; and our post

---

check. (Keto-Diastix are small plastic reagent strips that react by changing color if a drop of liquid placed on the test end contains glucose. Their original purpose is to test urine for the presence of glucose, but my parents adapted them into a tool for checking soda to make sure it didn't have any sugar in it).

took home the gold, First Place in Crime Prevention tactics, along with Fourth Place in Burglary in Progress response.

The most important thing I learned from the trip, though, came from that bottle of Lipton green tea. A new way to let the dragon drink without worrying about juice boxes. Now I use Gatorade (because it doesn't have high fructose corn syrup) which always makes me laugh at the irony: the drink that almost killed me as a baby, when my parents thought I was just sick, now helps me fight the dragon. And aside from learning about a new way to control hypoglycemia came the reassurance that even with the dragon inside of us, we can accomplish great things. We can pursue our dreams, despite the roadblocks and discrimination that may eventually arise because of diabetes; we can compete in physically demanding competitions, regardless of what other people say or think; we can even become a National Youth Rep for explorer posts across the country. The dragon may try to hold us back and keep us down, but we must rise up despite it, because of it, always looking for new and better ways to manage the beast and battle with it ardently, fervently. Victory lies always within our grasp; we need only reach for it, stretch out our hand and take it from the dragon, even though it may put up a fight. And when it does—just splash it with green tea.

Facing the Dragon's Fire

The sharp tones of my fire department pager jolted me awake, my heart racing at two o'clock in the morning. The dispatcher's steady voice crackled from the small black box as I jumped out of bed, pulling on my pants, and quickly checked my blood sugar. "WNKT502 Hanover Township Police to the Whippany and Cedar Knolls Fire Departments. You're responding to 1902 Long Hill Terrace in the backyard. Caller from Starling Place reports some sort of fire in the backyard at that address, possibly on the back porch. Repeating…" I didn't bother listening to him again as I ran down the stairs and looked up the street. 1902 Long Hill Terrace was just a few houses from mine.

"Oh, crap," I whispered under my breath as a huge plume of thick black smoke billowed into the night. I hopped in my car, wondering if I should run up the block, see if anyone was inside. I didn't have any of my gear, though, and we were told never to respond directly to the scene. With my blue lights activated, I drove as quickly as I could without being careless and flew into the station, putting on my bunker gear as other fire fighters arrived.

"It's a big one," I said. "I saw it. Mask up."

Adrenaline high, pulse through the roof. I'm going to fight a fire. My first actual fire. Feet in boots, pull up the suspenders, pull on the Nomex mask, slip my arms into my turnout coat. Uncap a bottle of Gatorade from my bunker pants pocket, drink it all (I was only 88 mg/dl when I checked myself) before pressing on my SCBA face mask, pulling the straps for a tight seal.

In the engine, we connected our air tanks—our SCBAs—and awaited orders from our lieutenant, listening for an update from the chief who just arrived on the scene. *"Confirmed working fire,"* he said over the radio. Didn't I just say that? *"Engine 81, hook up to the hydrant and lay in a line when you arrive."*

"Okay boys," our lieutenant said from the front seat, "we got a live one."

With the siren blaring, we zipped out of the firehouse bay and rocketed back to my street, waking up everyone along the way.

We hooked up to the hydrant across from my house as the driver slowly pulled up the street, the thick hose line dropping out of the back of the truck as we went. The Cedar Knolls ladder truck was already out front. Chief said over the radio to pull a line to the back of the house, start attacking the fire there. Then pull another line to the front door. Rescue operations were set into motion. Firefighters from Cedar Knolls erected a ladder to the bedroom window. Another lieutenant from Whippany went through the front door, but couldn't go far. We backed him up with another hose line, and I was three deep on it—three men away from the nozzle. The fire licked the ceiling over our heads, smoke filling the hallway and whatever parts of the living room we could see, devouring the house from the back to the front.

The bedroom was empty. Could the homeowner be away? Already with a neighbor? We fought the fire, spraying thousands of gallons of water onto the flames as they consumed everything in their path. Like the dragon's fire.

Then the air horn blasts came, reverberating through the neighborhood like trumpets of war. Three blasts. Evacuate the building. Too dangerous to stay inside. The roof was about to collapse. Too dangerous to continue any search and rescue. We backed out, down the steps, spraying water from the outside into the dragon's mouth.

Eventually the flames died down. There were still a few hotspots here and there. They assigned me the hose line in the backyard, aiming up through a window into the attic where a few tongues of flame still licked the roof. I remember that's when he said it over the radio. The lieutenant who first went into the house.

"206, we've got a body here. Front living room."

Only a few feet from where we were. A few feet from where I had crouched down, my knees on the floorboards, soaking up the runoff water that the fire didn't convert to steam.

I had to stop for a minute. Did I hear him right? A body?

EMS personnel screamed on the radio, what did they need, did they need a stretcher?

No. Already charred beyond recognition. Leave the body for the coroner.

Instinctively, I wanted to see it. I made my way to the front of the house after sufficiently dousing the hot spots in the attic. I walked past the other firefighters. Through the front door that I had crossed not two hours before. And caught a glance, looking at the charred wood of the living room. Saw the body burned and shriveled, arms and legs curled in. I said a quick prayer, hoping she (turns out it was an elderly woman, in her eighties, her children already moved to California or Florida or something) didn't suffer. Smoke inhalation would've knocked her out first, I reasoned along with the other firefighters when we attended the group counseling session a week later. She was likely already dead before we even arrived. Was she already asleep in her chair?

But we found her on the floor. What was she thinking? Was she afraid when she saw the flames engulfing her living room? Started by a tiki torch on her porch. Working smoke detectors might have saved her life, warned her before it was too late.

What if I had gone there instead of going to the firehouse? Could I have saved her?

No, they said. I had no gear. No equipment. I couldn't have done anything.

But the question still tickles the back of my mind. I could've tried. Maybe I could've saved her. Maybe I could've done something. I was so close...

Some people said I could never be a firefighter. I was a diabetic, how would that work? Would I just put the fire on hold, hit pause while I checked my blood sugar and took juice or gave myself a shot of insulin?

No, of course I couldn't do that. But I could take precautions. Keeping my diabetes well controlled; keeping Gatorade in the pockets of my bunker pants, making sure I drank some before going to a fire scene if I knew I'd be doing heavy work. The fire academy was tough, especially making sure I had the time to check myself before our lunch break and keeping Gatorade always close by. Sometimes the other kids (I took the Junior Firefighting program because I was only seventeen at the time—we did all the same things as the full program except power tools. We even did the live burn building training) would ask me what I was doing. "I'm a diabetic," I'd say. They'd nod, half-understanding.

After the first week of training, the class instructor designated me as one of the class leaders. I oversaw two platoons, making sure everyone got set up in the morning before live burn days, taking attendance, acting as the liaison to the course instructors if my classmates had questions or concerns.

Me. The diabetic kid as a class leader. I didn't let the dragon hold me back. Sure, some days—when we lugged hundred-pound hose lines wearing seventy pounds of gear for eight hours, or crawled around on our hands and knees with masks over our faces to simulate a search of a smoky room—those days, my blood sugar might drop to 40 and I'd need to take a break, drink a few more bottles of Gatorade. It would frustrate me. (I even pulled a muscle in my back and could barely walk, but that didn't have anything to do with the dragon—it just made all the practical exercises more excruciating). I would hate having to go to the bathroom to take a shot, or checking my blood sugar as fast as I could while everyone else ate, cutting into the time I had for my lunch.

But I got through it. My childhood dream—one of them, anyway—was to become a firefighter, and I did it. I graduated the academy as a class leader and went on to volunteer with my town as a fire fighter. I did everything every other fire fighter does, even though I am a diabetic. We can never let the dragon hold us down, because as soon as it does—it wins. And even though we lost one of the citizens we swore to protect that day in the Long Hill Terrace fire, I learned that we could get through the shock as a family, supporting one another and learning from the tragedy. Just as we can support each other as diabetics, lean on one another, and wrestle the dragon together.

PART III

❦ ❦ ❦ ❦ ✠ ✠ ✠ ❦ ❦ ❦ ❦

A DRAGON SLAYER'S FUTURE

The Next Big Step

After graduating from high school, I knew that college loomed on the horizon, along with the changes in lifestyle and independence that came with it. I decided to go to Seton Hall University and, preparing for my Pirate Adventure Orientation day in June, packed my bags for the overnight weekend every incoming freshman was required to attend. My dad dropped me off at the front gate, the security booth both reassuring and forbidding, an iron fence surrounding the school. I followed the campus map to the auditorium where I was scheduled to check-in and received my dorm assignment. The peer advisors were friendly enough, but I didn't want to be there. I was going to commute anyway, so why did I even have to do this? I really didn't need to know what the dorms were like. From the stories I'd heard, no one should have to subject themselves to that, even if it was just for one night.

I threw my bags in the small, cell-like room, checking to make sure I had all my diabetes supplies. No nurse's office here. I would have to take care of myself, a big change from grammar school and high school where the nurse was always minutes away to give me juice and keep my tester and supplies handy. Now, I'd have to carry everything myself.

No refrigerator here, either. Good thing it would only be for a few days. I had a few bottles of Gatorade and orange juice. That should last, I figured. Because if my blood sugar went low in the middle of the night, I wouldn't have anywhere to go. I'd be stuck without sugar, and then I could pass out...the scenarios all played out in my head, making me sweat already.

Consulting my orientation packet, I left the dorm before my roommate showed up. If I could have avoided him for the entire weekend, I wouldn't have been disappointed. I hoped for a while that they had assigned me to a dorm by myself, but I wasn't that lucky. I was always a loner and didn't care much for company.

They gave us our school-issued computers that day, and I was part of the University Honors Program so we got laptops with touch screens. It was my first experience with a tablet computing system, and I was beyond excited. I would play with the touchscreen even when I didn't have to, just because I could. I didn't even have a smart phone at the time. I had an iPod touch, but that was the extent of my technological advancement.

At lunch, I sat at a table by myself. Some other kids came

and sat with me, and we struck up a conversation. I left to give myself a shot of insulin, though, and they were all gone by the time I got back.

One of the deans spoke to us in the gymnasium, said something about how the next four years would be the most influential of our lives. "You'll go from this"—he pointed to a student dressed in jeans, a backpack, and a t-shirt—"to this." Someone else walked onto the stage, complete with a suit, briefcase, and spiffy tie. "That's what we do here at Seton Hall. We transform students into professionals." I was still a little skeptical. My cousin went to Seton Hall, and he was still looking for a full-time job, even with a Bachelor's degree. "You may meet your future husband or wife right here on this very campus," he went on. Maybe. I looked around for anyone cute. "But most importantly, you'll leave here with the knowledge and skills you'll need to succeed in life."

Sounded kind of generic to me, but I clapped along with everyone else. I just couldn't wait to get this weekend over with.

I attended a few sessions from the different colleges and departments. I thought for a while that I wanted to major in Criminal Justice, but I wasn't so sure anymore. I went to the English Department and met with the Chairperson. I still remember that meeting to this day. We sat in a small room with a couch and two leather chairs surrounded by bookshelves and the department mailboxes. She gave me and the three other interested students printouts of what the English major would require. I studied it and mentioned that I had already written a fantasy novel. With a smile, she said to email her the link where she could get a copy (it was self-published at the time), and I promised I would.

Still on the fence, I left the session but held onto the printout. It was what I would eventually use to sign up for classes when I decided to become an English major in the spring semester of my freshman year. In high school, I never dreamed of getting a degree in English—my plans were always to major in Criminal Justice despite my Language Arts teacher who always insisted that I pursue English. And not only did I become an English major, but I went on to get my Masters in English (again, something I never dreamed of at the time), despite some bumps along the way. The room in which I sat that day during Pirate Adventure would later be the same room in which I've typed out essays, studied for finals, and fallen asleep from the stress of three twenty-page papers due by the end of the week.

They even had a small fridge there, which I could've used for insulin, if I wanted to (though I was always afraid someone would take it, or throw it away). As a commuter, I've forgotten my insulin more than once at home. Those days, I had to go hungry, either eating a small salad or skipping lunch altogether. Or the days when I forgot my Lantus at home and couldn't just skip a meal, realizing it before class. My professors were always lenient, though, and understood when I told them I would be a little late because I forgot my medication.

Diabetics who dorm at college face different challenges, I'm sure. Like making sure you have a stash of supplies to last until you can restock. Or hoping your roommate isn't afraid of needles or thinks you're a druggie. Having a refrigerator to store spare insulin, a place to keep your glucometer so it doesn't get destroyed when your suite mates decide to throw a party. Keeping track of alcohol consumption (let's be real, it happens) to avoid a sugar crash later.

Some parents might be afraid to let their diabetic kids go off and dorm at school, and honestly, I can't say that I wouldn't be nervous myself. But the parents of every diabetic will eventually have to hand over the sword to their son or daughter and trust that he or she can continue the fight independently. Communication is key, and having a plan and battle strategy worked out beforehand is crucial to wrestling the dragon. With the way my dad has been overprotective of me since the day I was born, I could envision him having a nervous breakdown if I had decided to live on campus. But I also know that he would have supported my decision at the same time. He would've trusted me enough to know that I could fight the dragon on my own—and if I ever needed him, he'd be only a phone call away.

During the first night of Pirate Adventure, I went up to the top level of the school's parking deck and looked out toward the Manhattan skyline. The stars above me seemed infinite, speckling a black canvas with little dots of hope. This was the next big step in my future. Come September, I would officially be a college student, taking control of my life, forging my own path. I was a knight, now, with Excalibur in my hands. The dragon grumbled inside me, upset that I enjoyed such freedom. But I just laughed, spread my arms and looked up at the night sky. I might not have been able to fly like a dragon, but with the world in front of me and the beast behind me, I believed that nothing would ever hold me back.

A Gun and a Badge

When I made the phone call to the Union City Police Department, I could hear my pulse in my ears. A secretary answered from the Chief's Office and asked how she could help me.

"Hi, my name's Anthony Cunder. Can I speak to Lieutenant Facchini, please?"

She transferred me to his office.

"Lieutenant Facchini," a voice came over the phone.

"Hi, this is Anthony Cunder, and I'm calling to see whether you have any openings for Class II Police Officers[1]? I know Eddie Blue, he was a Class II with you guys and he told me to give you a call."

"I know Blue, he's a good kid. Of course, we're always looking to hire Class IIs. Did you just send an email about it?"

"Yes, I did."

"Yeah I just saw it. I'm going to email you a copy of the

---

[1] In New Jersey, a Class II Police Officer does the same job as a regular police officer, but just works fewer hours and is considered part-time rather than full-time (and doesn't get benefits)

application, and when you finish it just give me a call to come bring it in. Okay?"

"Yes, sounds good. Thank you."

"Alright, Anthony. Talk to you soon."

I finished the application within a week, ecstatic, believing this would be my best chance to fulfill my other childhood dream of becoming a police officer. I went to the Union City Police Department, dressed in my red button-down that was slightly too big and my red striped tie. Through the front door and into the small lobby, I peered beyond the glass partition that separated me from the police desk. "Can I help you?" an officer asked.

"I'm here to see Lieutenant Facchini? I have an appointment."

The officer made a phone call, then told me to ring the bell on the wall by a side door.

I pressed something that looked like a buzzer, but nothing happened.

"No, the bell," he said. "Next to the door."

"Oh. This one," I said, my face hot.

"What were you pressing?" he asked, laughing.

"I don't know, this thing here looked like it was a bell." I'm still not exactly sure what I had touched.

When I finally managed to find the intercom buzzer, a

woman's voice asked me who I was.

"Anthony Cunder, here to see Lieutenant Facchini."

"Okay, come right up."

I pushed the door open.

He seemed ordinary enough—not quite the imposing detective I had imagined. A thin build, clean shaven, dressed in jeans and sneakers with a gold badge clipped to his belt.

"Hey, how's it going?" he greeted. "Have a seat right here." He pointed to a chair next to his desk as I gripped my application packet and folder of documents. I hoped I had remembered everything. Birth certificate. High school diploma. Social Security card. Driver's license. Two years of income tax returns.

"You have everything there?" he asked. "I'll take that." He flipped through it. "Your name's Anthony too?" he said with a smile.

"Yes. I'm guessing so is yours?"

"Best name in the world."

"And I'm guessing you're Italian, too," I ventured.

"How'd you know?" he joked.

"I'm Italian too."

"Cunder?"

"When my ancestors came over from Italy, they chopped off the *i* at Ellis Island. It used to be *Cunderi.* Or *Cundari.*

Something like that."

"Bastards," he whispered under his breath. "Just kidding."

I laughed. "I know, they should've kept it."

He asked me a few questions about my background, then said, "Alright, everything looks good. I'll go through it, call your employers and references, and you'll hear back from me in about a month. Just so you know a little about the department, the Class IIs here start at $20 an hour and work a base schedule of twenty hours a week. State law says that's the maximum you guys can work, but we need you more than twenty hours so we give you overtime for anything extra. The Chief is very supportive of the program. I'm sure you've heard that from Eddie Blue. We have about thirty Class IIs right now. Any questions for me?"

"Nope, not right now. Thank you."

"Okay, Ant. I'll give you a call soon. I'm sure everything will check out."

We shook hands and I left with a bounce in my step. Finally, my dream was going to come true.

I got the call about a month later to schedule my psychological evaluation. I passed that without a problem. In fact, Lieutenant Facchini told me that out of all the years he's been doing background investigations, he's never seen an IQ score on the psych exam as high as mine. The next step would be the medical evaluation.

I thought I wouldn't have a problem with this.

Turns out, I was wrong.

I filled out the evaluation questionnaire in the Secaucus clinic's waiting room, going down the list, checking No for every box. No history of heart disease. No high cholesterol. Never smoked. Heart murmurs, Arthritis, Diptheria, Phlebitis, Anemia, Asthma—No, no, no.

Then came diabetes. I checked yes, nonchalantly. I had gone through the physical exam for the fire department, and it wasn't an issue with them. I always kept it under tight control, my doctor said I was in the top one percentile of diabetics across the country. No sweat.

I handed in the evaluation form and waited for the nurse to call me in. She took my height, weight, drew blood for lab work and I almost passed out. Not really, but I did ask to lie down on the bed instead of sitting up like she wanted me to. Vision test, hearing test, passed those without a problem.

She put me in another room and I waited for the doctor. He came in, carrying his clipboard and stethoscope. The cold metal burned my skin as he checked my breathing.

"No medical issues, right?" he asked.

Like vomit, I couldn't stop the words from coming up.

"Just diabetes," I said. I was always so used to saying it during every new medical examination.

He paused, reviewing my questionnaire. "Diabetes? Do you have a note from your doctor?"

"A note?"

"Saying you're fit for duty as a police officer."

Wasn't that supposed to be this quack's job?

"I didn't know I needed one. I keep it under tight control, my A1C is usually around six."

He rubbed his chin. "I don't know if I can certify you as a diabetic."

"You can't just fail me because I'm a diabetic." My heart started racing. Was this really happening? Was my best chance at becoming a police officer going to disappear because of my diabetes?

"I have to check, because I know there are certain disqualifying diseases. Like if you're blind."

Was this guy serious? Diabetes and blindness were two very different conditions.

"Diabetes isn't one of them. I can promise you that." I had my lawsuit already planned in my mind.

"Let me check. Hold on a minute. I just have to make a few phone calls."

I crinkled the paper on the examination table, the

crackles exploding in my fist.

This can't be happening, I thought. This was supposed to be easy.

He came back nearly twenty minutes later, a thick packet in his hand. "Your doctor will need to fill this out." It looked like fifty pages. "This is the standard evaluation for diabetics who are applying to law enforcement positions. It's put out by the American Diabetes Association. Once he completes it, just bring it back here and I can sign off on it."

Another doctor's appointment? I took the packet. "So I just call here again after I get this done so I can drop it off to you?"

"Sure, or fax it or mail it."

"I'll drop it off. Thanks."

I left, fuming, cursing my body, my diabetes, my fate. I wanted to fight the dragon right there for ruining my chances, my dreams, my life. Never before had diabetes impacted me so directly, so extremely, so excruciatingly. I wanted to punch the dragon, kick it, stab it with every needle I'd ever used on myself. I had just visited my endocrinologist for my quarterly appointment the prior week. Now I had to go back. I couldn't just drop this off, I'd need to set up an appointment to go over it with him.

It asked for my insulin regimen, my dosages, my

medications; my blood glucose test logs, copies of my eye examinations. It asked if I had normal vibratory testing with a 128 Hz tuning fork, normal testing with 10 gram Semmes-Weinstein monofilament and normal orthostatic blood pressure and pulse testing, whatever those meant.[1] It asked for my serum creatinine levels and whether I went for regular stress testing. (And the Secret Service never even gave me the chance to fill out paperwork like this, although I supposed it wouldn't have mattered anyway. They probably still would've failed me, even if my doctor filled out the packet and marked everything down as perfect).

It was more than I could handle, and I nearly broke down and gave up. There was no way I could get all this done. I called my endocrinologist's office and scheduled an appointment for the next available opening—in a few days. I saw one of the nurse practitioners and she took whatever measurements she could: pulse, blood pressure, jotted down my regimen and dosages. She'd leave a note for the doctor, and he would fill out the rest. He'd give me a call when it

---

[1] I've since looked up what those tests entail: vibratory testing is to measure one's ability to feel vibration in the toes (to make sure all of the nerves in the outer limbs are still functioning); monofilament testing similarly measures a patient's ability to feel sensation in the toes and is performed by poking a thin, flexible plastic strip into the pad of the big toe and asking if the patient can feel the pressure. The plastic strip (monofilament) bends when 10 grams of pressure are applied (which is the testing standard) so all tests are uniform.

was ready to be picked up.

Lieutenant Facchini called me the next day, asking what happened. Apparently the doctor's office in Secaucus had contacted him and said they couldn't certify me, so I explained the situation. "Alright, Ant, just keep me updated. Try to get it done as soon as possible, because we want to hire you by the end of the month."

I said that I would do my best.

The next week, I still hadn't heard from my endocrinologist. I contacted the office, asking when it might be ready. "He'll call you," the receptionist said, an edge in her voice.

Another few days. Still no phone call. Another message left with the receptionist.

Finally, I heard from them. "Hi, Anthony. You actually need to schedule an appointment with Dr. Melfi so he can review this with you. When would you like to come in?"

"As soon as possible."

For the third time, I went to Dr. Melfi's office. Two weeks had passed since my physical in Secaucus. We reviewed the sheet comprehensively, and he said he needed to get some records from Dr. Starkman, my old endocrinologist, because I had only recently transitioned to his office. He asked if I had gotten a stress test within the past year, and I said I had results from one that had been completed two years ago. Based on my level of control and my medical history, he said that should suffice. Everything else checked out okay, and he printed a letter certifying me as fit for duty as a law enforcement officer.

Lieutenant Facchini called me again the day that I had all of the paperwork completed, signed, and in hand. "Hey, Lieutenant. I was just about to call you. I got everything done today and I'm going back to Secaucus to drop it off. I apologize for this, I didn't think it would take this long."

"No, Ant, don't apologize. It's fine. The important thing is that we want you to come work for us. Don't worry about this. And listen, you need to come in on Wednesday at nine AM to get sworn in. Just bring whatever medical paperwork you have with you then. Okay?"

"Okay, sounds good. Thank you."

They still wanted to hire me. Even though I was a diabetic, they still thought I'd be good enough, despite the dragon doing its best to hold me back.

On Wednesday, March 11, 2015 I went to the Union City Police Department and was sworn in as a Class II Union City Police Officer. My dream of getting paid to wear a badge and serve as an officer finally came true, and before I had even turned twenty-three. I handed Lieutenant Facchini the enormous packet with Dr. Melfi's evaluations and recommendations. He tossed it onto his desk without even looking. To this day, I don't think he ever opened it.

A Knight's Academy

To be honest, I was slightly misleading in the last chapter. Before I was hired by the Union City Police Department, I served as a volunteer Deputy Sheriff with the Essex County Sheriff's Office for two years, graduating the police academy in April 2013. So I had already (sort of) lived my dream of becoming a law enforcement officer, though when I started working for Union City I was actually getting paid to do it.

Even as a volunteer, I had all the powers of a full police officer while on duty, so before I could start, I was required to attend a police academy that would give me the training and skills I needed to do the (volunteer) job safely, effectively, and professionally.

After a year-long application process that entailed its own psychological evaluation, physical fitness test, and medical exam (this time, completed by my own primary care physician), the academy approached at top speed: not a full-time, Monday-through-Friday academy—because I would only be certified as a Class II Special Law Enforcement Officer as a Deputy Sheriff—but an academy that met on

Tuesday, Wednesday and Thursday nights, as well as a full day on Saturdays for six-and-a-half months. I received the list of equipment I'd have to purchase as part of my training: khaki uniforms that made me look like a janitor; leather duty belt; gun holster; Sig Sauer P229 DAK .40 caliber handgun (we had to purchase our own weapons); handcuffs; fluorescent traffic vest; poncho for the rainy days; PR-24 nightstick; blue sweat pants and sweatshirts for our physical training; and a water bottle from Modell's among a list of about forty things, even including an athletic supporter and protective cup for the guys.

As the academy orientation day approached, I started to get both excited and nervous. I had heard stories about this day. Hell Day. The day the Drill Instructors tried to get people to quit. We'd have to endure hours of angry sergeants screaming in our faces, do push-ups until our arms fell off, run back and forth across the parking lot until our legs turned to water. Or so the stories said.

I drove down Route 46 on that September morning, the sun breaking over the horizon, reminding myself to call everybody *Sir* or *Ma'am.* I had some experience with police academies as a Law Enforcement Explorer with the Morris County Sheriff's Office when I was in high school. They hosted a week-long sleep-away boot camp that resembled everything we'd see in a real police academy. The screaming. The uniform inspections. The marching. The discipline. They even woke us up with fog horns at 2 am one morning to go for a jog around the parking lot. One kid was so dazed he stood at attention at the foot of his cot for a whole minute before we got him to understand that we had to get outside.

So I had some idea of what to expect. But not even that could have fully prepared me for what was about to come.

The recruits lined up in the parking lot, waiting for the instructors to come out at 8 am. We had our black gear bags at our feet. Our hats on our heads, our ties crisp and straightened, our uniforms pressed, our low-quarter shoes shined. The seconds ticked by. My heart pounded. Is this really what I wanted to do? I was volunteering for this, I wasn't even getting paid. In fact, I even had to pay my own academy tuition.

Then I thought of what graduation would be like, wearing a uniform and a badge like I had always dreamed of ever since I was a kid. And I decided that that was exactly where I wanted to be.

The doors burst open. "Bags up!" one DI yelled, his hat pulled down, nearly covering his eyes. "Get those bags up! Get them up! I don't want to see a single bag on the deck!"

I scooped up my bag. It probably weighed about seventy pounds with all my gear—everything I'd need for the entire six-month academy packed into a single duffel bag (towels for PT, sweat gear, duty gear, boots—EVERYTHING)—and held it close to my chest. I'd practiced a few techniques at home and learned that it was best to pull the bag as close to my body as possible. It felt lighter that way.

"Higher!" another DI yelled, her voice ferocious. "What do you think you're doing?" she screamed at someone down the line. I didn't turn my head. I couldn't look. I knew that much from the Explorers. Look straight ahead when standing at attention. Remain perfectly still. Do not move. Do not call attention to yourself.

Out of the corner of my eye, I saw someone's gear bag get dumped amid the screaming. I don't think he had a piece of gear that he was supposed to bring. "Now pick it all up and stow it properly, recruit!" the DI yelled.

"Bags down!" the first DI screamed, and we all dropped our bags, letting them hit the blacktop with relief. "WHAT WAS THAT?" the DI screamed. "You don't drop your gear! You put it down GENTLY! I don't want to hear your bags hit the deck a second time, or you'll be holding them until tomorrow! Now pick them up again!"

With a grimace, I bent down, grabbed the canvas fabric

and squeezed it, sweat already dripping down my back. I wondered what the dragon was thinking. If it would start to growl soon. If I'd have to call attention to myself and step out to drink some Gatorade. I didn't want to. I just wanted to blend in. I didn't want to get screamed at, even if I did have a medical excuse.

"Now move!" the DI screamed. "Run to this line." He pointed to a painted white line in the lot, and we all ran with our bags. "Now back!" he screamed when we got there. "Double time!" Back to the starting line. "Bags down! Hit the deck! Push-ups!" And we did push-ups until I felt like my arms really would fall off.

And we picked up our bags. And put them down. And ran. And did more push-ups. I looked down at one point and noticed that my finger had somehow started bleeding from the nail. Probably from gripping my gear bag so tightly. Then a woman DI came and started screaming in my face. Apparently it looked like I was smiling, or smirking. "You think something's funny, recruit?" she asked.

"Sir, no sir!"

As soon as the words left my mouth, I knew I was dead. And I had feared this moment, too. I wondered what would happen if I called the one female Drill Instructor *Sir* instead of *Ma'am*. I thought about it driving to the academy that morning. I jinxed myself.

"SIR? SIR?" I could feel her hot breath on my cheek.

"MA'AM, NO MA'AM!" I tried to save myself, screaming so loud my throat hurt.

"You think I'm a man?" she went on.

"Ma'am, no ma'am!"

"Get that bag higher!" I tried to lift it, but my arms were about to give out from fatigue. Other recruits had already dropped their bags, and I was about to.

But I couldn't. I couldn't let my dream die. I was here. At the police academy. The real police academy. This was what I wanted to do. So I lifted it higher. Not much higher, but it was enough.

She went on to the next recruit, and I prayed that it would all be over soon.

Finally, after what seemed like hours, they lined us up alphabetically so we could be assigned recruit numbers. I didn't want six. I knew I'd be near the top with a last name like Cunder, but I didn't want six. Anything but six. Call it superstitious, but I believed that bad things would come if I was given that number.

I tried to see how many recruits were before me. They had us count out loud.

"One!"

"Two!"

"Three!"

And when the guy to my left said "Six!" I couldn't help but smile.

I liked the number seven. Seven was a good number.

I thought that would be the end of the torture for the day, but I was wrong. We had a bit of a reprieve in the classroom where they went over academy procedures, and how the rest of our training would unfold. Then they brought us to the gym where we did more push-ups—all in our uniforms. They lined us up in the hallway and made us squat with our backs against the wall. Most of our uniforms were drenched.

Then back in the classroom where they gave us a booklet of rules and regulations and told us to copy the entire thing— verbatim—by hand by next Saturday, when the first day of our training would officially start. The academy Commanding Officer, Captain Lori Apicelli, gave us our instructions: "If you make a mistake on a page, rewrite the whole thing. No white out, no cross-outs. Use yellow legal-paper and blue ink. Everything must be copied exactly. If you see a logo, draw the logo. If you see a bullet point, use a bullet point. If you see a page number, write the page number. At the top of each page, you also have to include your name, recruit number, and department. We're going to be reading all of these to make sure you followed directions, and if we see a mistake, you'll be writing the whole thing again."

I made a few mistakes when I started the assignment that night. Some were at the very bottom of the page, so I had to crumple it up and write the whole page again. I probably went through about eighty sheets of paper. And I still had homework from my college classes to finish, too. I questioned my judgement a bit—how was I supposed to get through two semesters (twelve credits each) of college *and* a six-month police academy *and* wrestle the dragon on top of it all?

I thought about just leaving some mistakes. But it's a good thing I didn't, because Captain Apicelli was true to her word. Turns out, when it came time for us to hand in our assignments, only I and one other recruit had actually used legal-sized paper. Everyone else had used 8.5 X 11. And they all had to copy the forty-page booklet again.

I told the academy staff on orientation day that I was a diabetic and would need to bring my medication with me. They asked for a note from my doctor, and I called and got one the next day. Everyone had to have a water bottle, and I got two. One filled with water, the other with Gatorade. And for some unfathomable reason, I had an affinity for the yellow Gatorade. Most of the instructors accepted my special case without question. If I ever needed to take a break during physical training, I just stepped aside. (I'll be honest, there were certain times I was grateful for a low blood sugar so I could take a break and watch the other recruits suffer as they punched out thirty push-ups and fifty mountain climbers while I got to rest and sip my Gatorade).

A guest instructor made an appearance one night, though, an instructor known for his brutality. Ours was the first recruit class that didn't have to face him as a full-time instructor, and he made up for his retirement with vengeance. Some rumors suggested that he was forced to leave by the Police Training Commission because of his unconventional tactics. Like when he ran the recruits into the ground—literally—making them do pushups outside during a thunderstorm in three inches of muddy water. Luckily, we avoided that. But I didn't escape his gaze. He noticed my clear plastic water bottle filled with something other than water.

"Recruit!" he screamed in my face as I stood at attention, the glare of the gymnasium lights blinding me.

"Sir, yes sir!" I yelled. I was sick that day, too. A wicked cold had plagued me all week, and my head was pounding.

"What is that, recruit?" He pointed to the bottle.

"Sir, Gatorade, sir! I'm a diabetic."

"Sarge, he's good," our regular instructor said, trying to ease his wrath.

But, like the dragon, he was not easily appeased.

"How do I know that's Gatorade?" he asked me.

I stayed quiet, looking straight ahead, not moving.

"How do I know you didn't piss in your bottle?"

I must admit, it was kind of funny. But not in the moment, with the hot breath of a fiery drill sergeant blasting in my face.

"Sir, you don't, sir!"

He stared at me. I don't know if that was the response he wanted. Or the one he was expecting. Maybe he felt bad for me because I had a disability. For some reason, I don't think so.

Eventually he moved on, and I did my best to blend into the class again. That's one thing I learned in the police academy. Standing out was never a good thing. Better to just melt into the crowd, don't be the best, don't be the worst, don't be different. Because the ones who were different were usually the ones who got the extra push-ups.

Some people told us that we'd miss the academy when the six months were over. I thought they were crazy, but I've since realized they were right. Partly, anyway. I didn't miss the screaming and the yelling, but I did miss the other recruits with whom I literally sweat and bled for the past six months. Some of us stayed in touch, but most have since drifted away, to other departments, continuing on with their lives and leaving the academy behind.

Our last night together—graduation night—came as one final hoorah for Essex County College Police Academy SLEO Class 12-1. And it was probably one of the proudest moments of my life. Putting on the uniform and walking up to receive my certificate with friends and families cheering me on made Hell Day entirely worth it. I graduated first in my class with the highest academic average, managed to get all A's in my college classes too, and kept my blood sugar in (relatively) good range through it all.

Despite the Drill Instructors who tried to get us to quit; despite the absence of a social life for six months; despite the dragon roaring at me and trying to keep me down, I finally realized my childhood dream of becoming a duly sworn and certified law enforcement officer, and in that moment, I couldn't be happier.

Mononucleosis:

Diabetic Style

I shouldn't have taken the extra shift. Sure, it was going to be a great paycheck with the overtime, but it was my fourth full day working, and the next morning I'd have to be up early for an academic conference in New Hampshire.

"I'm sorry, sir, the road is closed," I said to a motorist trying to bypass the barricades in Union City.

"What's going on?" he asked, sticking his nose out the window.

"Earth day celebration," I answered, brushing invisible specks of dirt off my uniform.

"Oh. I can't get through there?"

Did he not see the huge stage in the middle of the road? The popcorn stand, the vendor tables? "No, sir. The road is closed."

He made a face at me, like I just ruined his day by telling him he couldn't drive down New York Avenue, and spun his car around. I pulled the Tropicana orange juice bottle from my back pocket and took a sip, warding off the impending low blood sugar I felt crawling around inside me. I grimaced as I swallowed, the beginnings of a sore throat scratching at my esophagus. I shouldn't have taken the overtime. I should've just gone home after my eight-hour shift. Working from 8 AM until 10 PM was not a good idea, and now I was getting sick.

Performers came, gave speeches about Earth Day and why it was special. When the event started winding down, the day darkening into night, my sergeant told me to cut off the lines at the popcorn and concession stands. Some kids came up, tried to get in line, but I had to tell them "No more, sorry." A pang of sympathy shot through me when I saw their faces, their puppy dog eyes pulling at my heart strings. But I had to get home, I couldn't stay there all night, and my sergeant did say…

"Alright, you guys can be the last ones," I finally relented, ushering them in front of me.

Eventually the crowds thinned, and I got the last bag of popcorn. Probably not the best idea: the salt stung the inside of my throat, and the dry kernels tore at my inflamed tonsil. It felt like knives were stabbing the inside of my neck, and I had to press my fingers against the left side of my throat just to swallow.

But I pushed through. I went home, got up at six o'clock the next morning to drive up to New Hampshire. The dragon laughed at me when I checked my blood sugar—it was 64 mg/dl. I'd have to eat something, even though my throat burned. I barely slept the night before, tossing and turning, the dragon growling the whole time.

Never before did I imagine that eating a bowl of cereal could be so painful. This was more than a simple sore throat, but I crossed my fingers and hoped it would go away on its own. Hopefully it was just from a lack of sleep, from working so much the past week. Yeah, that's it, I told myself.

I slept during most of the six-hour drive to the conference, though it was by no means a peaceful sleep. Every bump and twist in the road yanked me out of whatever shallow slumber I had managed to find. Each time I swallowed, I cringed, massaging my throat—but to no avail.

"AJ, are you okay?" my boyfriend Kyle asked while he drove us up to New Hampshire—he was part of Seton Hall's Graduate English program and would be presenting a paper at the conference too.

"Fine," I mumbled. "Don't know how I'm going to present my paper at this thing, though. Hopefully I'm better by tomorrow."

Keene State University welcomed us, and the hotel was decent enough. I collapsed on the bed and didn't want to move, pressing my face into the cold pillow. Kyle said something, but I couldn't even understand him.

At the opening ceremonies, the poet laureate gave his speech, read his customary medieval poem. My professor glanced over at me slumped in my chair and asked if I was okay.

"Fine," I said, regurgitating my automatic response even as the dragon writhed. Did the beast do this to me?

She knew I wasn't, though. After the ceremonies, she gave me a Motrin, and that helped a bit but didn't do much to cool the fire burning my throat. I opened my mouth in front of our bathroom mirror and nearly passed out. My left tonsil looked like it could burst at any moment, and white puss spots speckled the engorged gland. I couldn't eat. Swallowing spit was painful. And the dragon laughed every time my blood sugar dipped, forcing me to drink something, eat something to regulate my diabetes.

I curled up in the bed, hot and cold at the same time, pulling on the blankets then throwing them off. Kyle tried to find me Naked smoothies, the only thing (I thought) I'd be able to eat without too much pain. But they were like the Holy Grail, elusive in New Hampshire. Eventually he found something similar, and I took small sips of the cool, thick liquid, letting it just trickle down my throat.

I didn't last much longer. I told my professor that I couldn't stay. I wouldn't be able to survive without eating, let alone read my paper aloud at the conference. Kyle took me home the next morning—a Sunday—another six-hour drive—and I went to an Emergency Care clinic. I almost went to the hospital, but I really do hate hospitals.

The office spun around me, and I started sweating. The doctor finally came in—I don't even know if he was a doctor, or just a nurse, or med student, or technician— peering into my mouth, humming to himself.

"Oh yeah," he said. "Your tonsil is huge," he muttered.

"Do you think it could be strep?" I asked.

"Could be. We'll do a swab."

I hated those. My gag reflexes were horrible, and I had to just think happy thoughts when he jabbed the cotton swab down my throat.

Little did I know, I'd have to put up with a lot more than that pretty soon.

"We'll get these results back in a few minutes." He walked out, and I wondered if this was how my parents felt when they waited for the results of my pee test in my pediatrician's office all those years ago.

Turns out it wasn't strep. "This came back negative," he said, "but we'll send it to the lab just to make sure. In the meantime, we'll take a blood test to see if you have mono."

My heart beat faster. "Mono?" No, I couldn't have mono. The horror stories I had heard of that disease… My cousin had it once, and he was sick for a month. "How could I have mono?"

"Most young adults get it at some point. And once you get it, you'll never get it again, so that's always a good thing."

Sure, if I survived it.

They took my blood and sent me home, telling me to gargle salt water twice a day and take ibuprofen for the pain.

It didn't work though. In fact, it got worse. And through it all, I had to manage my blood sugar, make sure I took my insulin—but not too much insulin, because then I'd have to eat something and want to rip my throat out.

The office called the next day. I did have mono. I did some research online, found that corticosteroid medication often helped with the inflammation. So they prescribed me prednisone—but only a day's worth. It helped, but two days later, I had to go back. I went to the office and the tech looked in my mouth. The inflammation had gotten worse.

It was a woman this time, and she seemed a bit more

knowledgeable. "You've got a peritonsular abscess here," she said, frowning.

"What does that mean?" I asked. It certainly didn't sound good.

"An infected tonsil. I'm going to have to press on it to try and drain some of the liquid building up in there."

Oh God. Not another swab in my throat.

She pressed. My eyes teared up. I gagged. She pulled out quickly.

"Sorry," I said. "My gag reflexes are horrible." And I felt the pus draining down my throat, leaking out of my inflamed, infected tonsil. Gross.

"Here's a garbage pail," she said. "In case you throw up. I have to try a bit more, though, or you'll have to go to the hospital and have it drained surgically."

"Like…how?"

"They'll drain it with a needle."

I almost fainted. "No, let's just do it this way."

Once. Twice. Three more times, and then she said she wouldn't do anymore. I don't think she wanted to risk getting vomit on her. She didn't want to provoke the dragon anymore.

"If it doesn't get better, you'll have to go see an ENT."

"ENT?"

"Ears, nose, throat doctor."

"Oh, okay." I got a bigger prednisone prescription, with the warning that it would raise my blood sugar.

I didn't care about that. As long as it wouldn't make me go low and force me to eat, I'd take it.

Thankfully, it worked. The swelling went down, and, even though mononucleosis is supposed to knock you out for a month, I was back at work in a few days.

I hope I never experience a sore throat like that again. I was almost tempted to go to the hospital and just have my tonsils removed—but I think my fear of surgery outweighed whatever pain I felt. As a diabetic, though, I had the additional struggle of making sure, throughout it all, my blood sugar was regulated. Normally, low blood sugars are the easiest to treat. Drink some juice, have something to eat, and we're good to go. But when you can't swallow, it becomes one of the most difficult things in the world.

The same goes for when I would have a stomach virus as a kid. Eating something, taking insulin, and then throwing it up moments later—it becomes a problem when you need that food to prevent hypoglycemia. I wish I had an easy answer or a better solution, but the truth is, fighting an illness and the dragon at the same time is going to be difficult no matter what you do. In situations like mine, or with a sickness that involves vomiting or difficulty eating, sometimes it's better to take less insulin, even if it means running high for a few days. High blood sugar can be corrected with a shot, but if you can't eat or drink—or keep that food in your stomach—then a low blood sugar could be immediately dangerous.

I'm just grateful that—hopefully—I'll never have to endure mono like that again. Whether it had anything to do with my working the extra shift, or not getting enough sleep, or something that was going to happen anyway, I'll never know. I do know, though, that fighting two battles with the dragon breathing down my neck is not and never will be an easy experience.

A Day in the Life of... Me

Diabetics can live normal lives. And if you have any doubt of that, I've decided to include a chapter to prove it.

When it's still dark out, and I'm snuggled under my warm blankets, I never want to get out of bed. When my alarm goes off at 5:45 AM for work, I don't want to get up. Sometimes, I wish that I had a job that would let me just work from home, get up whenever I wanted, drink a cup of hot tea in the morning and just watch TV to flush the drowsiness from my body. I heard someone on the radio talk about his morning routine, how he has to get up early to make it to the studio on time. One morning, when he was particularly tired, he sat at the edge of his bed and had to repeat to himself, "I can do this." That was his mantra, and I've since borrowed it on a few occasions.

So I pull myself up, shuffle to the kitchen and check my blood sugar—give myself a shot if I'm a little high, or drink some juice if I'm low. I may have an apple or a banana, but usually I don't eat anything when I first wake up. I get dressed, pack my backpack, grab a bottle of water and make sure I have enough bottles of orange juice and a Gatorade in case my blood sugar goes low while I'm working. I make sure I have my cell phone, my insulin, my wallet. There have been times when I forgot a needle for my insulin pen, or took a pen with only ten units left in it. Needless to say, the dragon got the better of me on those days, and I went hungry. (Once I didn't realize that I had forgotten a pen needle until after I already ate. I wasn't sure what to do. Would the pharmacy have needles? I went to the Walgreens and had to call my doctor's office for a prescription. It took a while, but eventually it went through. Cost me forty bucks for two boxes of pen needles, but it was a lesson learned. Now, I keep an extra bag of pen needles and alcohol swabs in my bag in case of emergency.)

Then comes the dreaded commute that always snarls me in work traffic—I don't have to be at the police department until 7:30 AM, but if I don't leave by 6:30 I won't make it there until 8:30 with all the traffic heading into New York City. Unfortunately, I have to take the same highways that lead to the George Washington Bridge, the Lincoln Tunnel, and the Holland Tunnel, so there's no escaping the mass of vehicles. And when I finally reach Union City, finding a parking space is another disaster. They don't offer employee parking, so we have to find a spot on the street just like everyone else. It's taken me twenty minutes to find a space before.

At headquarters, I'll sign in, get my equipment, check my department email for any memos or special orders, then sign out a police car and head to my assignment as a School Resource Officer during the school year, or wait until line-up for an assignment during the summer. My first school is an elementary school, and I always have a blast with George, one of the security guards. His goal in life is to prank as many people as he can: he always waves his hand at a teacher down the hall as if he's calling her over, and then when she walks all that way, he just says how warm it is—he was just fanning himself, no, he doesn't need anything from her. And that's just one of his tricks (I can't give them all away).

I get my buttered roll from the corner deli and give myself a shot of insulin in the bathroom. That's sometimes a pain, especially if there are people waiting (it's just a single person bathroom for faculty at the school). For a while, I wasn't sure where I could give myself a shot without having to take off my entire duty belt, or pulling up my shirt and then struggling to tuck it back in. Eventually, I figured out I could just roll up my uniform sleeve and give myself a shot in the arm. That's been working out well, though with long sleeves sometimes it's a hassle to get it rolled all the way up.

With breakfast out of the way, I make my rounds through

the school, making sure it's safe and secure and giving the kids high-fives when they see me walking in the hallway. Then I head to my next school—this one's for high school kids, but it's an annex to the main Union City High School, so there are only about one hundred students. The security guards are a blast here too, along with the custodial staff, and sometimes there's food in the conference room. If it looks really good, I'll have some of it and take another shot of insulin. One security guard is a type II diabetic, and we've talked about how we each wrestle the dragon, how he's struggled to find the right insulin dose to keep his sugar from going high in the morning, or from going too low. He passed out, once, and broke his ribs, so his fight with the dragon has been more difficult than mine.

And there's the security guard who hates when other teachers and faculty take his coffee or milk. He's gotten so angry that he's even sabotaged the carton of milk he brought by dumping old creamers in it along with sink water. (I think the secretary who would always take it learned her lesson and started bringing her own.)

Then comes my favorite time of the day: lunch! It's a tough choice, sometimes, whether I want to get pizza and garlic knots, or grab a tuna salad on a bagel with American cheese from Dunkin Donuts, or a turkey sub from Blimpie, or a sandwich from Fiji's deli. Whatever my decision, I'll check my blood sugar in the police car and either give myself a shot right there (I worry, sometimes, that someone walking by will see me injecting myself in the arm and say something about it, but it hasn't happened yet. One person did come up to the car and start asking me something while I still had the needle in me, but he didn't seem fazed by it. I answered his question (something about if he would get arrested if he took a flower after a woman said he could—he wasn't entirely coherent, and was probably drunk) and he went on his way) or I'll go to a bathroom (if there's one available, like at Blimpie or Dunkin Donuts).

My last school of the day isn't quite as fun as the other two. But I get through it—I make my rounds, inspect the school to make sure it complies with state fire codes (there was a fire at that school in 2016, so fire safety is a top priority for me while I'm there). At dismissal, I stand by one of the side street exits and make sure kids don't run across the street into traffic. 3:00 PM comes, and I head back to the station to sign out, complete any paperwork or reports, and then at 3:30 dive into rush hour traffic. Sometimes I just miss it, and then other times—like when there's an accident—I'm sitting in traffic for two hours when the commute should take only twenty minutes. I get back to my apartment, check my blood sugar to make sure I corrected accurately for my lunch, take my once-a-day basal insulin (I've since switched to Tresiba, after my insurance company said they would no longer cover Lantus), take a shower, then either take a nap if it was a stressful day, go to the gym if I need to get a workout in (making sure I check my blood sugar before exercising and taking a bottle of Gatorade with me to catch any lows while on the gym floor), or do some creative writing.

Dinner consists of me either coming home and cooking, or getting Panera after the gym, or sometimes just throwing something quick into the oven like a chicken patty (along with the customary carb count and insulin calculation. Some meals have become so routine that I already know how much insulin I need to take without having to add everything up). Then I'll plop down on the couch and watch Netflix or Hulu and wind down until it's time to snuggle back under the covers to repeat the whole process again the next day.

Normal. Ordinary. Routine.

Diabetic.

As normal, ordinary, and routine as anyone else's day. There are some days, though, when I just can't seem to keep my blood sugar up or down. One day, no matter how much juice I drank, I kept going low. I even ate spoonfuls of syrup (and it wasn't the sugar-free kind) and I still couldn't stay over 75 mg/dl. I didn't know why it was happening—I didn't exercise that day, and I didn't take any more insulin than usual. It was just a quirk, another oddity of the dragon we have to battle.

But most days are ordinary, for me—at least, what has become my ordinary. Sure, there are days when I've helped the U.S. Marshals catch a fugitive sex offender, or assisted our detective bureau with the bust of a drug and gambling ring, or secured a scene while the FBI raided a local pharmacy; or when I had to arrest a student for bringing a pellet gun to school, or break up a fight between a mother and her knife-wielding daughter; or shivered at the thrill that shot through me on my first day of patrol after graduating from the police academy—but most days are uneventful, normal, just like most days fighting the dragon are routine. That doesn't mean there aren't highs and lows (figuratively and literally), but everyone has their own highs and lows, diabetics and non-diabetics alike.

Thankfully, the technology we have today gives us better tools and weapons to fight the dragon—to live lives like anyone else. That's not to say our battle is easy, though. A closed-loop insulin system—one that monitors blood sugar, administers insulin, regulates highs and lows—is close, according to contemporary research. The Medtronic 670G

Closed Loop pump is already on the market and automatically adjusts insulin delivery based on blood sugar data via a continuous glucose monitor. Those like me, though, who hate the thought of being attached to a machine for the rest of my life, must continue to inject and monitor glucose the "old fashioned" way. That's not to say additional improvements and advancements won't come down the pipeline. On the contrary, I'm sure they will, all the while working towards that elusive cure that will banish the dragon for good.

Until that time, though, we must continue to fight. We must continue to chase our dreams, and support one another, and lean on one another. We must battle together and face this dragon—and our fears—with courage and resolution. We must not fear our difference—what sets us apart from others. Rather, we must embrace it. It is what makes us unique—what makes us who we are. It strengthens us, unites us, and gives us the armor we need to face whatever life throws our way. In battling the dragon, we know that we can overcome any obstacle, succeed in any challenge, hurdle any chasm. Even when people discriminate against us—like the Secret Service did to me—we have to stand up and show them that they're wrong. Maybe a lawsuit will be able to do that. Maybe it won't. Either way, I have two choices (as we all do): I can give up on my dreams because of the dragon, or I can persevere and move forward. I choose the latter, and in doing so, I win the fight against the dragon.

Whatever your feelings about the beast, do not let it overcome you. Do not give up. Our medication and our decisions to eat nutritious foods and exercise are what make us strong, like the ambrosia and nectar of the gods. Take your insulin—your antidote—and you can conquer the world. Refuse it, and the dragon will consume you. I could have refused to take my insulin while at the police academy, or while in school. But if I didn't take my medicine, my mind would've gone fuzzy, my muscles may have stopped working. I wouldn't have done well on my tests, and I might not have even graduated—the academy or college—at all. I wouldn't have been able to realize my dream of becoming a police officer. I wouldn't have passed the medical review (for Union City, anyway). I might have already lost a limb if I refused to monitor my diabetes, with the dragon inside me for so long. I might not have been able to write this book, with the complications that come from poor diabetes management. I certainly wouldn't be able to live as I live and do what I do if I hadn't wrestled the dragon as diligently as I have and as I continue to do.

Even now, when I'm not working as a School Resource

Officer and I'm walking the beat, I keep a bottle of orange juice in my back pocket. People ask me about it. They give me strange looks. But it's something I must do, because it could be disastrous if my sugar goes low when I'm searching a house for a burglary suspect. Or if I'm directing traffic at the scene of a multi-vehicle crash during rush hour. Or if I'm struggling with someone resisting arrest who just swung at one of my fellow officers. Diabetes hasn't held me back from living my dreams (for the most part), but only because I wake up every morning and fight the dragon. If I ever stop, even for just one day, it could literally be the death of me. Passing out because of low blood sugar in the middle of the street with a firearm on my belt while an anti-law enforcement sentiment pervades this country's political climate could be deadly. But, just like I don't let the criminals win when they try to fight against the law, I don't let the dragon win. Ever.

A Final Message

As I diabetic, I consider myself fortunate that I was diagnosed as an infant. I can't remember a life without the dragon; I avoided the devastating transition so many diabetics go through when they're diagnosed as teenagers and young adults—during such formative and hormone-filled years that are tough in their own right. I can't imagine what it must be like to suddenly find yourself faced with a new world, a new way of life, a new battle you must fight every day. I can't imagine what it must be like to face the dragon for the first time when so many other battles rage around you. I can't imagine what that struggle must feel like.

I've heard stories from acquaintances who were diagnosed during those years, or have children who were diagnosed as young adults. Stories of kids who refuse to take their shots because they're afraid of being different. Afraid that their friends won't like them anymore because they're diabetics. Afraid of losing the love of their family because of the dragon, or afraid they won't find love themselves. I thought that myself for a while—that I might not find love because of the dragon—but I've found someone who I've been with for over three years, someone who understands the battles I fight and supports me through them. Who reminds me to take my once-a-day shot when I forget, or wakes me up at night when I'm sweaty and tells me to check my blood sugar to make sure I'm not low. Who loves me for who I am, and—even though he hates needles—never backs down from fighting the dragon with me.

I've heard stories of diabetics who feel like the world is collapsing around them, feeling the heat of the dragon's fire as it breathes down your neck. Every injection, every time someone asks about your pump, every time someone asks what you're doing when you prick your finger and check your blood sugar, know you are not alone in your fight. We all fight together in our battle against the dragon until science finds a cure.

I can promise you that I have never felt any less loved because of my disease. I can't promise that it will always be easy, and I won't say I never felt embarrassed or awkward when I had to check my sugar or take an injection in front of people I'd just met, or absolutely devastated when the Secret Service discriminated against me and crushed my hopes because of the dragon. But I just have to shut out my discomfort for a moment and do what I need to do because I refuse to let the dragon win. As soon as I don't take my medicine or cave in to embarrassment, or let the world end because of one reviewing physician's bias and prejudice, the dragon gains the upper hand, and my disease suddenly controls me. I will never let that happen. And, if nothing else, it becomes a talking point. I can explain that, no, I'm not injecting a pre-filled heroin syringe. I'm actually a diabetic, and I have been since I was seventeen-months-old. And despite my disease, I've never once stopped living—or chasing—my dreams. Until the day I die, I will never let diabetes hold me back. And you shouldn't let it hold you back either.

If you ever need someone to talk to, reach out to me at ajcunder.author@gmail.com or on Twitter @aj_cunder, or online at www.WrestlingTheDragon.com. I will do my best to answer every email or message. Facebook has a bunch of support groups too, such as *Type 1 Diabetes Support Group* where I'm an active member, or groups that cover both type I and type II like *Diabetes Support.* You can also reach out to your local chapter of the Juvenile Diabetes Research Foundation or American Diabetes Association. Attend walks and fundraiser events to network and meet with other people who fight the dragon too. I've had great experiences at the walks I've gone to, and I've met a bunch of great people and support groups. Visit the ADA's website at diabetes.org or the JDRF at jdrf.org for more information. The ADA in particular has a vast array of online resources such as online communities for people who were recently diagnosed, those who love someone with diabetes, who recount their experience living with type I or type II diabetes, or who think they might be diabetic. There are recipes, meal planning guides, ways to take action and support diabetes research, and a list of upcoming events. It's a resource I wish I had taken advantage of sooner, so please visit the website and see how it can help you.

When I say in the title of this book that I've fought diabetes and won, I don't mean that in the sense that I somehow no longer have diabetes. For us type I diabetics (for now), that's impossible. When I say that I've won, I mean it in the sense that I refuse to let it conquer me despite the dragon's best efforts. I win against my disease because I control it—I don't let it control me. I win every day that I wake up and do what I want to do despite my diabetes— every day I take my medicine; every day I smile and live and laugh and love. Because together, even if it seems impossible, we can succeed in our fight against the dragon. As long as we never give up and never give in, the dragon will never win.

Appendix A

(Or Should I Say

Pancreas?)

Just a few more tidbits (in no particular order) about my experience with diabetes that didn't fit elsewhere in the book.

➤ Trying to explain the difference between type I and type II diabetes. I feel like diabetics (and doctors) are really the only ones who seem to fully understand how two diseases so similar in their effects can at the same time differ so greatly. And, on the same note, explaining to people who think I'm diabetic because of my diet and lifestyle choices (which isn't even entirely accurate—or the only contributing factors—for type II diabetes either) that type I diabetes is purely genetic, has nothing to do with diet or exercise, and can't be cured or alleviated in any way except through medication.

≫⁺ Dealing with the night (and day) sweats of low blood sugar. Like, seriously, why must my body secrete what seems like every last drop of moisture when my blood sugar goes low? I suppose it's as good a warning mechanism as any. Except when I'm sitting in class, or taking a test, and my shirt suddenly becomes see-through. Oh yeah. It's happened.

≫⁺ Restraining myself from eating the entire refrigerator or pantry or cupboard when the hypoglycemic munchies kick in. And coping with the bloated stomach that inevitably ensues after consuming enormous quantities of food. Trying to explain this feeling to others when they ask, and telling them it feels like I haven't eaten in weeks. "What does it feel like?" everyone wants to know. "Hungry. Dizzy. Hungry. Lethargic. Still hungry. Like I'll eat an entire pizza and cake and five sandwiches."

≫⁺ Telling people who say I can't have sugar that, actually, I can—as long as I take my medicine. Or if my blood sugar is low. (And wondering in the back of my mind where these people earned their medical degrees…)

»→ Stockpiling medical supplies at the insistence of my father in case we ever lost our insurance. I probably have enough lancets and alcohol swabs and pen cap needles to last a few years. All my supplies fill up an entire bedroom dresser. And making sure I'll be home when the shipment arrives so the insulin doesn't stay outside in the heat of summer or cold of winter for too long. Once, no one was home and FedEx took the package back to their storage facility. We went to get it the next day, as soon as we could, and found that it had been left outside. The ice packs were all melted. My dad called the insurance company, and they argued with him—they didn't want to give us a new order of insulin despite the fact that all of the insulin could have spoiled. Eventually he worked his magic, and they listened.

»→ Feeling simultaneously guilty and grateful when my Great-Aunt Margie (with whom I was very close) was diagnosed with type II diabetes. I was thankful that, finally, I had someone like me in my family who would know what it was like to check her blood sugar every day and watch what she ate (this was back when I was on the two-shots-a-day regimen with NPH and Humalog, when I actually couldn't have sugar any time I wanted). My grandmother on my father's side was also a type II diabetic, but we never really spent as much time with her as I did with my Aunt Margie—my Anma, as I would call her as a child. The name stuck, and to this day I still call her that.

»→ Carrying a Gatorade or orange juice bottle in my back pocket wherever I go—and the comments from people who I meet for the first time. "What, our drinks aren't good enough for you?" Kyle's aunt teased me the first time I went up to meet his family. "No, I'm a diabetic," I answered with a laugh. She apologized profusely, and I knew she had said it in jest. The dragon apparently wasn't appeased, though—she was diagnosed with type II diabetes a year later.

»→ Moments of delusional fantasy when my blood sugar would continuously go low throughout an entire day and I would think that somehow my diabetes had been miraculously cured. *The insulin is making me just go low now*, I would think to myself. I don't need to take it anymore! Of course I hadn't been cured. It was just a quirk.

»→ Other odd quirks. Like if I exercise in the morning, I need to take insulin. Yup, you read that correctly.

Consistently, if I wake up and my blood sugar is near 100 mg/dl and I then go exercise vigorously without eating or drinking anything but water, my blood sugar will invariably be in the high 200s afterwards. Don't know why. My doctor can't seem to explain it. Just something I have to deal with. Or when I'm working, I'll cover for a meal—two slices of pizza and a diet Snapple—and my blood sugar will be 279 mg/dl when I get home. The next day, I'll do the same thing, the same amount of physical activity, eat the same food, and give myself four extra units to try to compensate for it—and my blood sugar will be 52 mg/dl when I get home. The dragon can be so finicky, sometimes.

»→ Worrying about whether my glucose meter is too hot or cold or if I have spare batteries. There have been times in the winter when I left it in the car and couldn't use it because it said it needed to warm up. Who knew that a glucose meter needed mittens?

»→ When I was younger, my dad would leave a whistle by my bedside in case I went low in the middle of the night. Rather than get out of bed, I'd blow the whistle and he'd know that I felt low. I'd plug my ears with my fingers and blow on the whistle as hard as I could, especially if it was morning and I knew he'd already be up and downstairs. Once, (I think I was in sixth grade) he got really angry that I blew the whistle. "You can come downstairs and get your own juice," he said. I never blew the whistle again.

⟫⁺ The fear of passing on the dragon to my kids, if I ever have biological children.

⟫⁺ Coping with the extreme anxiety that comes with low blood sugar. And the irritability. Trying to control it and not let it impact my relationships.

⟫⁺ Remembering my med alert bracelet, so everyone will know that I'm chained to the dragon. I had a rainbow bracelet—and still do—from when I was in first grade that clipped around my wrist. (One of my good friends, Angela Weisl—also my co-author, beta reader, and former professor—once thought that it was a Pride bracelet!) At my quarterly endocrinologist appointments, Dr. Starkman would always check to make sure I wore it, but sometimes I'd forget. Not that I hated wearing it, I just wouldn't always remember, and I'd be embarrassed when he asked to see my wrist and it was bare. It made me feel naked.

⟫⁺ Explaining to everyone who asks (including my doctor) why I don't want to use a pump. It's just a personal preference, really, but I don't like the idea of being permanently attached to a machine, even if it can make fighting the dragon easier. I'd rather take my shots, and my control is already very tight.

»⁺ Remembering whether I took my once-a-day shot. There have been times where I truly could not remember if I took it or not, and I wasn't sure if I should just take an injection in case I didn't or wait a few hours to see if my blood sugar levels rise. If I ever can't remember, I'll usually wait to see how my blood sugar reacts.

»⁺ I will only use one brand of cotton balls for my glucose testing: the ones in the blue bag from ShopRite. In my opinion, they're the softest, and feel like actual cotton. I hate the acrylic ones that my parents used to get sometimes. Those would just smear the blood anyway rather than absorb it.

»⁺ I also avoid using my left ring finger to check my blood sugar because I can never get it to stop bleeding if I do. I heard once that the tradition of wearing a wedding band on the left ring finger emerged because of a vein that goes all the way from the heart to the tip of that finger. Based on my experience, I believe it. The only way I can stop the bleeding is if I hold my finger under cold water for a few minutes.

»→ Always taking my own lancet device to the doctor's when I go for my appointment. The lancet devices they have at the office always hurt, I've been told, and I learned my lesson after using it once. Trust me. Take your own.

»→ Learning that "sugar free" never really means sugar free. A lot of sugar free candies still have carbohydrates, which the body processes as sugar—just not as quickly. I always used to eat sugar free candy when I was younger, but I've since stopped. Diet sodas are still okay, as long as you don't mind the artificial sweetener.

»→ The "insulin before" or "insulin after" meals debate. Fast-acting insulin is supposed to work within minutes according to the manufacturer and according to my doctor. But for me, it seems to take at least thirty minutes to an hour to really take effect. This has always prompted me to take an injection before I ate and just make an educated guess as to what I'm going to be hungry for. Sometimes it works out, sometimes it doesn't. Sometimes I do wait until after I eat, especially if I'm a little low before a meal, though, and sometimes, when I take a shot first—even if I don't know exactly what I'm going to have—I'll give myself three more units of insulin for whatever "extra" I might want.

➤ Resenting having to get blood drawn for a simple A1C test. My old endocrinologist's office had a machine that could calculate an A1C with a single drop of blood from a finger prick. It's time my current endocrinologist purchased one of those machines…

Appendix (Pancreas) B

Some tips for wrestling the dragon from my own experience.

(DISCLAIMER: Please do not substitute this book for medical advice from a qualified healthcare provider. The best way to manage your diabetes is to follow the plan you have discussed with your doctor, endocrinologist, or diabetes educator. The following is simply a list of practices and habits I've used to maintain tight control of my disease. Please do not start or stop anything in your own regimen without first consulting your physician. If you or a loved one are experiencing any of the symptoms outlined in this book and are not already diagnosed as a diabetic, please see a doctor or go to the hospital right away and ask them to perform a blood glucose test. It could save your life.)

I won't say that we're lucky to have diabetes. It certainly can be taxing, at times. However, diabetes is at least something we can control. We can fight it and win—successfully—every time. Every diabetic can live a long, healthy life as long as he or she consistently monitors glucose and takes medication. People who are diagnosed with cancer, or chronic obstructive pulmonary disease, or coronary artery disease, or AIDS, have a much higher likelihood of death because technology has not yet found the tools necessary to guarantee a successful fight. Those who have Downs syndrome, or lose an arm or a leg, or have some other permanent physical deformity don't have the opportunity or the tools that we have as diabetics to overcome their disabilities.

That's not to say that the dragon can't be a deadly foe— diabetes certainly can be deadly if not monitored closely. According to the American Diabetes Association, diabetes affected 29.1 million Americans in 2012, with 1.4 million new cases annually. Of the nearly 30 million, only 21 million were officially diagnosed. The other 8.1 million were living with diabetes and did not even know it. There are an estimated 208,000 kids in America under the age of twenty who have diagnosed diabetes. Globally, the World Health Organization estimates 422 million as having diabetes in 2014, up from 108 million in 1980. In 2012, an estimated 1.5 million deaths were directly caused by diabetes, while another 2.2 million deaths arose from high blood glucose.

Complications that can arise from failure to maintain effective control include hypertension, high cholesterol, cardiovascular disease, an increased risk for heart attack or stroke, diabetic retinopathy (which can lead to vision problems and blindness), kidney disease, and limb amputations. In my opinion, I'd rather take the time to check my blood sugar and take my medication than risk such devastating complications. But that's just me.

The following is a list of what I do to keep my A1C consistently under 7.0%. My hope is that it will be helpful to others too.

» • Check your blood sugar. It's tough to fight the dragon when you have no idea where it is. You wouldn't go into a boxing match with a blindfold, so why try to manage your diabetes without knowing exactly what you have to fight? I check myself at least four times every day— always in the morning when I wake up and at night before I go to bed—and before each meal. My parents came up with a system to rotate through my fingers so one or two fingers don't get over-used. On even days, I use my right hand; odd days, I use my left; I start with my thumb for the first blood sugar check of the day and then work towards my pinky. Usually I don't have to double up on a finger, but there are days where I check myself more than five times. On those days, I'll either use a finger from my other hand or I'll use a thicker finger (like my thumb or pointer finger) twice.

»→ Take your medication. Just like a knight would be foolish to battle a dragon without a sword, it's impossible to maintain control of your diabetes without taking the medication prescribed by your physician (especially for type I diabetics. For type II, a doctor may recommend controlling the disease with diet and exercise). I've never once intentionally missed an injection (though there have certainly been times when I've forgotten to take it). And I know for those of you on injections, it may feel redundant to have to take two shots at the same time, but there are times when I want to eat something or my blood sugar is a little high at the same time I take my Tresiba (basal) shot. Taking a second injection isn't fun, but it's just something I have to do.

»→ Always carry Gatorade, or glucose tablets, or some form of fast-acting sugar with you at all times. As my dad always said, any good strategy for fighting diabetes is two-pronged: you have to fight the lows and the highs, and the easiest way to fight the dragon's low growls is to have sugar on you. If you don't like Gatorade, maybe you like orange juice, or apple juice, or cranberry juice. Healthy sugars are the best, but if you really despise all of it, then drinks like sweetened iced tea can do the trick.

➺ Keep a log of your blood sugars and insulin dosages, along with what you eat. My dad used to keep a log religiously for years, and I still have them stockpiled in my diabetes cabinet. Every blood sugar, every insulin injection with the dosage, every meal would go into the log. For those of you who are finding it difficult to pin down an effective strategy, this can be a good way for you to communicate with your doctor and troubleshoot areas that are giving you a tough time. Maybe you find yourself going low or high in the morning. Keeping track of what you eat the night before, how much insulin you take, what your blood sugar was at bedtime can help explain what's going on and you can figure out what to do to combat it.

❖ There are several good mobile applications available that can help with this. I like using OneDrop—it lets me log my glucose, my insulin dosage, my carb intake, and my activity level all on one easy screen. And it also lets me share a log of all that data with my doctor. I find electronic logging much easier than carrying around a physical paper and pen. Easier to organize the data, and much more convenient overall.

➺ Be cautions of when you eat fatty foods like

cheeseburgers or steaks. I've found (and my doctor has corroborated) that the body converts fat into glucose much later than pure sugar or carbohydrates, requiring me to monitor my glucose levels closely during the seven-to-ten hours after eating such foods. There have been times when I've eaten a cheeseburger for dinner at 5 PM, checked my sugar before bed at 9 (when it was within my target range), then woke up at 3 AM with a blood sugar in the 300s. Of course the simple solution is to avoid eating a lot of fats. That would be the healthy option. But sometimes, you just can't resist...

➤ Meet with your doctor regularly to go over your plan and regimen. He or she can answer any questions you have about your diabetes management and you can discuss options to tighten your control even more.

➤ Don't be embarrassed. I know it's hard sometimes, especially with a new diagnosis. But it really isn't anything to be ashamed of. This is our fight, and if people don't like you because of it, then they aren't true friends.

➤ Never give up. Don't let the dragon win. We have every opportunity in the world to live long, healthy, happy lives. With technology, we have the tools we need to beat the dragon every day. We just have to keep fighting. Our burden is just different. Like my dad always says, EVERYONE has a burden. The dragon just happens to be ours.

Additional Resources

I know I've mentioned a few already, but here's a list of websites and resources to help anyone struggling with diabetes (or friends and family members too):

»→ The American Diabetes Association's website at www.diabetes.org or @AmDiabetesAssn (on Twitter) offers resources like a self-risk assessment, an overview of Diabetes Basics, Advocacy groups, diabetes events and activities in your community, and guidelines for healthy living with diabetes.

»→ The Juvenile Diabetes Research Foundation, an organization focused more intently on type I diabetes at www.jdrf.org or @JDRF. There are opportunities to get involved, stay up to date on the latest news and developments in diabetes research, and find support groups.

»→ The International Diabetes Foundation at www.idf.org or @IntDiabetesFed. With a global approach to diabetes care and prevention, the IDF offers a worldwide network of members, publications, and resources, hosting events like the IDF Congress in places like Abu Dhabi, UAE and campaigns to promote access to improved diabetes care in areas like Brazil and South America.

➻ At www.DiabetesDaily.com (also @diabetesdaily) you can "Learn," "Ask," and "Eat"—okay, maybe you can't exactly *eat* on their website, but it does offer a comprehensive list of diabetes-friendly recipes that you can sort by "Course," "Type of diet," and "Ingredients." You can also find upcoming diabetes-related events in your community and interact with thousands of other diabetics on their community forum pages

➻ Camp Nejeda at www.campnejeda.org where kids with type I diabetes can attend a summer sleep away camp with other diabetics without having to worry about fitting in, taking insulin shots, or checking their blood glucose. From the Camp Nejeda website: "Camp Nejeda has been providing empowering summer camp and other programs for children with type 1 diabetes and their families since 1958. In addition to providing eight weeks of traditional Summer Sleep-Away camp, Camp Nejeda offers Family Camps, Day Camps, Spring and Fall weekend programs, T1D Adult Weekend, Nurse Education seminars and much more." Located in Sussex County, NJ, the camp might be too far for some of you, however you can search www.childrenwithdiabetes.com

for camps across the United States (and even Canada) to find one in your area.

≫→ www.EatGoodCarbs.com, a website run by Johann Burani MS, RD, CDE who has over twenty-five years of experience in nutritional counseling, offers recipes and explains the difference between carbs that cause a rapid rise in blood sugar versus the slowly-digested carbs that keep you full longer and don't spike blood glucose. You can also find links to healthy-living books, presentations on the Glycemic Index, and dietary options tailored to diabetics.

≫→ Search "Diabetes Support" on Facebook and you will find a few good support groups. I can say the ones I've been active on (Like Type 1 Diabetes Support) are truly amazing. The sense of community and camaraderie between fellow diabetics is incredibly encouraging, and people share their own tips, tricks, and experiences #WrestlingTheDragon. So come join! Maybe I'll see you there.

≫→ At www.WrestlingTheDragon.com, my own website, (or @aj_cunder on Twitter) you can learn more about how I've overcome diabetes and wrestled the dragon inside me. I've also compiled a quick-access list of all the links to the resources mentioned here.

About the Author

AJ graduated from Seton Hall University with a Master of Arts in English (and a concentration in Creative Writing) after receiving his Bachelor of Arts in English and Philosophy also from Seton Hall. When he was sixteen, he joined the Whippany Fire Department as a volunteer,  serving as a fire fighter in every capacity despite having diabetes. In the Fall of 2012, while maintaining a full-time college course load, he began the Essex County Public Safety Training Academy's Basic Course for Class II Special Law Enforcement Officers, graduating in April 2013 with the highest academic average (and earning a 4.0 GPA in both Fall and Spring college semesters as well). Afterwards, he served as a Deputy Sheriff with the Essex County Sheriff's Office for two years until he was hired by the Union City Police Department as a Class II Police Officer in March of 2015.

As a writer, he has published short fiction in a variety of online and print journals and magazines. His genre-bending work "The Last Will and Testament of Harry B. Balsagna" was selected as a finalist in *Permafrost Magazine*'s 2017 New Alchemy contest, and his work appears or is forthcoming in *Harpur Palate*, *NAILED Magazine*, *Rose Red Review*, *Quantum Fairy Tales*, *Flash Fiction Magazine*, and *Breath & Shadow* (a quarterly journal of disability culture and literature). He has also published two fantasy novels, *The Silver Talon* and its sequel, *Destiny's Map: The Lost Road*, and has co-authored an introductory book on the literature of the Middle Ages as part of Routledge's Basics Series.

While not reading or writing, he enjoys practicing medieval swordplay with friends, attending Renaissance Fairs, visiting the Medieval galleries and displays of museums, playing the piano, and spending time at the gym. Visit his website at www.WrestlingTheDragon.com.

89296005R00150

Made in the USA
Columbia, SC
19 February 2018